Recapturing the Mind of Christ

Copyright © 2009 Michele Barnes McClendon. All Rights Reserved.

Scripture taken from the Holy Bible, New International Version. Copyright © 1973, 1978, 1984 International Bible Society. Used by permission of Zondervan Bible Publishers. All rights reserved.

For Sunshine
I miss you.

And for Dianna.

CONTENTS

Acknowledgments	3
Introduction	4
Chapter 1: Resplendent Renewal	7
Chapter 2: Breath of Reluctance, Wind of Change	14
Chapter 3: Joanna's Pearl	25
Chapter 4: A Visible Sign	34
Chapter 5: Black and Plain	41
Chapter 6: One Small Obedient Thing	47
Chapter 7: A Soul's Profit	54
Chapter 8: A Sign to the Angels and Man	61
Chapter 9: Obedience and Cultural Comfort	66
Chapter 10: Signs of Godly Femininity	73
Chapter 11: Men Folk on the Journey	80
Chapter 12: The Wide-Eyed Ride	88
Chapter 13: It Takes a Village to Raise a Movement	96
Bibliography/Reference	101

ACKNOWLEDGMENTS

Endless thanks to the eight women who offered their voices to this effort. Without courage there can be no candor. God's grace to each of you.

Deepest thanks to my husband who patiently listened to my frustrations while writing this book, and who spurred me on from start to finish. I am blessed beyond measure that you are my husband. I iuka you.

Heartfelt thanks to my mother who never stops supporting my writing endeavors; to Beth Mismas, Tracy Preston and Christie Gustafson who lend endless support and encouragement. Everyone should have friends as faithful as you.

To my dear sons: thank you for your patience and resilient tenderness as I pecked away at the keyboard. Even though Mama is also a writer, you will always be my most important job. I pray to God I never fail you. I love you more deeply than you can know.

INTRODUCTION

This is a book I never meant to write. I didn't choose the story; rather, it chose me. It is a story that began to write itself (and sought to drag me along) when our odd and unexplainable experiences began to materialize and take form in one another. One woman here, another there, and wait – another one back down that way – we all felt the distinct urgency to cover our heads for God. We were just ordinary women who happened to love God. We were minding our own business – going to work, standing in line at the grocery store, changing diapers, making dinner, mad at our hips for being too wide, tossing in a load of laundry, and enjoying our fair share of joys while denying our insecurities. We were wives, mothers, single women, students, career women and desperate dieters. Some of us were too vain. Some of us would tell it like it is, and others of us would bite our tongue. We had bad hair days and root canals and too many of us were often late for church. We were just real women, in all our glory, who happened to love God and wanted to be faithful and obedient. That was all.

Then one day something happened to us. We were met with an experience that threatened to upset our otherwise normal lives. Many of us never saw it coming. We had the unmistakable feeling that we were supposed to cover our heads. To some, that meant covering during prayer; to others, it meant covering during church worship services. Still others felt led to cover all the time, citing the I Thessalonians 5:17 charge to pray (and therefore *cover*) without ceasing.

We wondered what was going on. Wasn't head covering for the Amish? Mennonites? Why should *we* feel such an urgency to cover our heads? We hadn't even heard so much as a sermon on it! But wait...there *was* that one passage in the Bible that mentioned women covering their heads. What was it ... I Corinthians or II Corinthians or something? Sure, most of us recalled that passage, but we reasoned (and most likely were taught) that this passage was no longer relevant in today's culture. That was then, this is now. Besides, our hair was our natural covering anyway, right? *Right?*

Some of us lost sleep over it. Some of us upset our spouses over it. We took the sideways glances and swallowed hard. "God help me," we thought. "I *must* do this."

If you picked up this book, chances are you have at least a small bit of interest in head covering. Maybe you want to better understand a friend or sister who covers her head. Maybe you are a husband who is trying to get his mind around his wife's peculiar new practice.

Or maybe you're a woman who has thought about it once or twice yourself. Maybe the idea of it came to you, but you quickly dismissed it. Maybe you tried talking about it with a friend or two, but nobody thought it was very important. Maybe someone told you that our liberty in Christ means we no longer have to be bound by such things. We don't need to wear some silly head covering in this day and age. Maybe you sighed and nodded in agreement. Perhaps that was enough, and maybe you don't need to cover. This book is not about telling you how wrong you are if you choose *not* to cover. But if you are a bit curious about head covering, or have felt compelled to cover your own head, then perhaps you have the right book in hand. The perspectives of the women in this book are not the perspectives of women who have all the answers. While I've included the unique stories of covering women from a range of different backgrounds, it should not be assumed that I necessarily subscribe to the viewpoints represented in each account. But these were important stories that needed to be told. My hope is that each chronicle will speak to someone who needs to hear it. But ours is no perfect tapestry of voices. To be sure, each of us has her own history, and we live daily with our own reality. We are human and we are flawed. We don't think we have it all right while everyone else has it all wrong. Please don't misunderstand us. Most of us never meant to walk this path; we were quite comfortable where we were in our lives. Some of us weren't entirely sure we were even being called to cover. We had some doubts. We had our questions. We did our fair share of ducking and dodging the head covering bullet. We were sometimes reluctant, but we wanted desperately to please and honor God. So in the end, we concluded that if we were to err, we would prefer to err on the side of obedience and let the chips fall where they may.

And now we'd like to invite you to our journey.

Chapter 1

Resplendent Renewal

Charm is deceptive, and beauty is fleeting; but a woman who fears the Lord is to be praised. – Proverbs 31:30

In almost any age, at any given point, physical beauty has been held at a high standard, particularly where women are concerned. In both our current age and in past generations, we can look almost anywhere and see a beautiful woman: magazines, billboards, cereal boxes, car advertisements, album covers – and all this before the internet even reared its ubiquitous head. With the advent of the internet, there is now no end to the number of beautiful women we can see. We can hardly check our email without seeing advertisements of once "ugly" women made beautiful when their lips are made fuller or their wrinkles are smoothed out. Being beautiful is good. We gain friends, career opportunities, and popularity in our social lives; beautiful spouses, beautiful children, and beautiful homes. Indeed, being beautiful is part of the "good life" many aspire to. We don't see it as any different, really, than our aspirations for material or career success. If we work very hard, make the right connections and invest in the right things, we think that sooner or later we'll be successful. Likewise, if we exercise enough, diet enough, get our lips injected enough, tan enough or wear physically revealing clothing often enough, sooner or later – if in even some small way – we will be beautiful.

Acceptance Through Beauty

In our pursuit of beauty, it seems many of us never stop long enough to ask ourselves *why* we really want to be beautiful. In my own life, beauty was a means to acceptance. If I looked good enough, showed my slender figure and waistline often enough, people would think me beautiful and then accept me. And if they accepted me, they would love me. And if people loved me, then I would have value. And if I had value, then I *mattered*. Youthful beauty at any cost is the brazen message of our culture, and it touts that nothing, neither old nor unattractive, matters very much. And everyone wants to matter.

This false message of beauty has found itself on the Christian's doorstep. We mistake it for a package that has our best interest at heart and so we open it up and consume its distorted truths. Far too many of us have grown up in churches or in Christian families where this flawed beauty standard is the norm, is happily approved and, along with material success, is even viewed as a sign of God's favor. As Christians we often say that we care about the marginalized, the weak, and the poor; but too often our actions demonstrate that we care more about the beautiful and the successful. These are the ones we align ourselves with. Far too often these are the ones we most eagerly accept.

It's no wonder so many Christian women zealously pursue physical beauty: professionally done nails, countless trips to the hair salon, visits to day spas and endless shopping trips, creams, fragrances, firming lotions and cosmetics – all in the name of looking or feeling beautiful. We simply cannot ignore the message that we must be beautiful and more specifically, thin and beautiful, to be acceptable.

Knowing and Living

In our present culture, the pursuit of beauty even in Christian circles is the norm. After all, it won Esther the throne, right? To be sure, there is nothing inherently wrong with wanting to be or look beautiful. But our current culture has placed such a great emphasis on youth and beauty, the soaring standards of which are nearly impossible to attain. Still, we work feverishly to reach them, often neglecting the eternal value of inner beauty. Far too often we fail to see the larger purposes God has for us as women. We know that our physical beauty is temporal (Proverbs 31:30), but many of us seem far more interested in others' acceptance of us than we are in living with a view to eternity. We know that the inner beauty of a gentle and quiet spirit is far more valuable to God than physical beauty (I Peter 3:3-4), but with our actions we live as though physical beauty is the more noble pursuit. Our knowing is not our living. Our believing doesn't flesh itself out in the decisions we make about beauty or the ways we judge beauty. Neither are we terribly concerned about our apathetic attitudes about beauty; we no longer even blush when we see a woman in a bikini or one scantily clad in a lingerie commercial. God calls our gray hair a crown of splendor (Proverbs 16:31), but we are told it is unattractive and therefore must be dyed. Were there times that I remembered this Bible passage, but still colored my hair anyway? Unfortunately, yes. I embraced the message of the world more than I embraced the message of my Heavenly Father. I'm ashamed to say that, but it's true. It's very hard going against the grain of the culture; it's so much easier to fit in. But to many, it's an exhausting and endless effort.

The Beautiful Rescue of God

I've heard it said that the Holy Spirit is the consummate Gentleman; He's not pushy and He won't twist your arm. He gently reminds and He delicately nudges and He quietly waits. His tender nudges often come softly during the course of our day, or in a movie, the content of which directs our attention to certain spiritual parallels, or in the word of a friend who senses our weariness. Somehow, some way, God makes provisions to rescue those of us who need rescuing the most. He does it in big ways – like when He sent His Son Jesus to die for the sins we couldn't save ourselves from. And He does it in small ways, too, like a thoughtfully written card from a friend or a meal offered in the warmth of hospitality.

And He rescues us in practical, everyday, normal-as-coffee ways through His Word. Like when a verse we've read a thousand times suddenly speaks to us like it never has before. Romans 12:1-2, for example: *Therefore, I urge you, brothers, in view of God's mercy, to offer your bodies as living sacrifices, holy and pleasing to God – this is your spiritual act of worship. Do not conform any longer to the pattern of this world, but be transformed by the renewing of your mind. Then you will be able to test and approve what God's will is – his good, pleasing and perfect will.*

After I'd made the decision to cover, this passage of Scripture spoke to me like never before. There are other passages, too – some we read often, others we may read only once in a while –but we take for granted that we understand its meaning and are rightly living that meaning out. This is particularly true of the head covering passage of Scripture found in I Corinthians 11:1-16. As a college freshman and

10

new Christian, I was taught that this passage of Scripture was no longer applicable today, and that it was relevant only to the culture of Paul's day. I shrugged it off and never missed a happy little evangelical beat. After all, head covering, submission, authority – these weren't things that were being talked about in the church I went to, anyway. I've read that same passage many times since the days of being a new believer and it always made me a tad uncomfortable. But I wasn't exactly sure why.

Over the years I would come to find that my church wasn't alone: many Christian churches taught that the I Corinthians passage was no longer relevant in today's culture, and consequently many faithful, God-loving people believed this passage just didn't pertain to them. Many never gave it a second thought. After all, that was then. This is now.

A Virtuous Truth

But something began to happen. Something began to unwind. Here, there and seemingly everywhere, a number of women began to raise questions about the relevance of this passage in today's culture. To be sure, many people – both men and women – have raised questions about this passage in the past. There were many who never subscribed to the message that this passage holds no meaning or value today. Apparently, enough people took issue with popular reasoning to write numerous books on the pertinence of this passage. There were and are a good number of books comprised of scriptural discourse on the topic of head covering, as well as in-depth studies on the validity of this passage.

But for many, like me, there was something larger going on here. Our perception of ourselves was beginning to change. Something beautiful

11

was unfolding, and it had nothing to do with the way we looked. Instead, it had everything to do with refocusing our vision in order to see things the way God sees them. Many of us felt we had aligned our thinking with the culture's thinking for too long. We now began to ask new questions about headship, order and submission. We began to ask new questions about beauty. We began to imagine living a life where love for Christ reigned supreme and where acceptance and love were no longer based on the old code. We began to imagine the grand possibility that we no longer had to be bound by someone else's truth. Could virtue and beauty be found in covering, instead of exposing? Might it dwell in submission rather than resistance? Could it be nestled in humility instead of pride? Would it dare show itself in relinquishing rather than holding tightly?

Many of us were infused with the desire to cover our heads and our bodies as well – Black women, White women, women from various places over the entire globe. Many of us found ourselves smack dab in the middle of what seemed to be a spiritual (re)awakening, of sorts. Our decision to cover our heads and dress modestly flies in the face of a sexualized culture, but brings us new dignity and hope. We glory in God's words written through the apostle Paul to the Corinthians: *Therefore we do not lose heart. Though outwardly we are wasting away, yet inwardly we are being renewed day by day. For our light and momentary troubles are achieving for us an eternal glory that far outweighs them all. So we fix our eyes not on what is seen, but on what is unseen. For what is seen is temporary, but what is unseen is eternal* (II Corinthians 4:16-18). Indeed, the truth of God's Word has replenished us. We are resplendently renewed and our once foggy spiritual vision is growing clearer.

Most women who choose to cover don't claim to have the market cornered on answering the great mysteries of the faith. To be sure, the wounds and fractures we've incurred in a flawed system of beauty don't just disappear overnight. And there are plenty of days we struggle and need encouraging reminders on why we are walking the journey of covering. But we are living a new reality now. And we keep moving forward.

Chapter 2

Breath of Reluctance, Wind of Change

A bruised reed he will not break, and a smoldering wick he will not snuff out. – Isaiah 42:3a

I couldn't stop thinking about it. At night I would lie awake in bed, picking apart the whole idea of it. I was looking for a loop hole: something, *anything,* that meant I didn't have to do this; something that might suggest that this was for some other woman, maybe, but certainly not for me.

I kept it to myself for as long as I could. Sooner or later, a husband has to know about such things. How come I never saw this coming? How come I'm afraid of this thing and excited about it at the same time? I needed time – more time – to sort this whole thing out. Head covering? Really, now, come on. Me?

I'd been fooling around on You Tube trying to find new and interesting ways to wear my head wrap. This head wrap idea was new for me, but it worked well: an Afro-centric and stylish way to transition from a straight perm back to my coarsely textured hair. It was delightfully convenient when I didn't feel like bothering with my hair (which was often), but I also enjoyed the versatility of the wrap and, wanting to find different ways to wrap it, decided to peruse head wrap tutorials on You Tube.

A few clicks of the mouse and somehow I stumbled upon videos of Christian women who cover their heads. Some of them were kind enough to do head covering tutorials on You Tube, and they weren't Amish or Mennonite women either. I kept watching. I listened as they talked about head covering, dressing modestly and wanting to honor their husbands. Some even said they keep their heads covered all the time. Before long I forgot about finding new ways to wear my head wrap. I was far more engrossed with these women who covered their heads. Gradually I began to feel a weight in the pit of my stomach. Something akin to conviction slowly settled there. I tried to ignore it, but I kept clicking to find more Christian women who cover their heads and weren't afraid to talk about it.

Once I had finished watching the tutorials, I sat there quietly for a few minutes. Inwardly I chided myself, "Why am I so concerned? This doesn't have anything to do with me. I'm acting like *I'm* about to start covering my head or something. Yeah, right." The weight in my stomach began to widen and move up toward my chest, bubbling up into a strange mixture of fear and excitement. I felt undeniably attracted to this form of faith profession. I had to know more.

I spent more hours than I care to say looking up information online about Christian women who cover their heads. I was amazed to find a community of these women online! "This is crazy," I thought to myself, but now I knew there was no way I could talk myself out of it. Finally honest with myself, I had to admit that I felt God might be speaking to me about covering my head.

The Scripture that Picked a Fight

The women I read about online often referred to I Corinthians 11:1-16 as the scriptural support for their head covering. I'd been a Christian for nearly 20 years, so I knew the passage they spoke of. I had always been taught (and so believed) that this passage was no longer relevant for our culture and that a woman's hair was her natural 'covering'. I had always felt divided and uncertain about that passage, however, and my tattered 18-year-old Bible bore the evidence: in the otherwise well-underlined, scribbled, highlighted, bracketed, arrowed, margin-written pages of my Bible, that lonely passage of scripture was as unmarked as it was the day my mother gave it to me. This told me – or rather, *reminded* me – that I'd never been fully convinced that this passage held no cultural relevance for today. I wasn't so sure that I believed it didn't apply to me. So for me, this passage had merely been set aside. It just never seemed important enough to return to.

But now I found myself dealing with it. I began to study the passage and try to see it with fresh eyes. I emailed my pastor, who sent me a small group of sermons that he had preached on this passage. I told him I thought I was feeling led to cover my head. He told me that it wasn't necessary for today, that it was a culture's way of demonstrating submission to authority back in biblical times, and that this would be done differently today. I asked him, in essence, if it would be alright for me to cover anyway, if I felt led. He told me that he appreciated my heart, but that I didn't need to wear a head covering. After this exchange, I was really confused.

I began to really dig my heels into praying about it. I wanted to forget about the whole thing, but I just couldn't get any peace about walking away from it. The head covering women I'd found online all seemed so sure, so strong, so devoted to God. One woman's website exhorted married women feeling led to cover to talk it out fully with their husbands. But I knew my husband. He would think it less than sensible and that his poor wife had come unhinged.

But I talked to him anyway. We looked at the passage in I Corinthians together, and talked about what it meant to us and how each of us interpreted it. He also seemed to think that this passage was no longer relevant for today's culture, and that from his understanding, a woman's hair appeared to act as a covering for her. I sighed. "Well, I don't know," I admitted. "I'm still trying to get peace about all of this. I'm not sure. Would you pray for me?" He smiled. "Yes, sweetie. I will." He was trying to be kind, trying to tread gently. But I knew what he must be thinking: "First vegetarianism, and now *this*? Is there no end to what this woman thinks is necessary?" And perhaps followed by the thought, "Why can't I just be *enough* for her?"

When my husband walked out of my upstairs office, I buried my face in my hands. I had absolutely no idea what I was going to do, and I had even less of an idea how I managed to get myself into such messes. Why couldn't I just be a *normal* Christian? I went to bed sad and uncertain.

The Doubt that Bit the Dust

But something happened overnight. Literally. When I woke up that Saturday morning, I remember thinking to myself, "I've got to do it. That's it. I can't turn around. I can't go back." Maybe God was leading me and maybe He wasn't, but I decided that I would rather err on the side of obedience than to walk a different path. I started a blog to chronicle my journey, and I slowly began to gain a following. I ardently read articles on head covering sites and the blogs of other Christian head covering women. I was astounded that there were so many of us out there.

The more I learned about head covering, the more I seemed to learn about myself. My conversion to head covering was followed closely by my conversion to dressing more modestly. Those who know me well know that I am not the woman walking around with plunging necklines or very short skirts. And though I may be considered a modest dresser by the standards of American culture, I got the very real sense that along with covering my head, I was to readjust my attire and cover more.

Some might wonder why I thought this necessary. But I began to give some attention to the reasons *why* I dressed the way I dressed. I began asking myself some tough questions like, "What's my motive for dressing the way I do?" or, "Do I think about God's glory when I put something on or stand in line to purchase it? Or do I think about my *own* glory and the attention that I will draw to myself when I wear it?" or, "Am I choosing clothes that will flatter my figure and highlight all my positives, and if so, *why?*" and, "How do my heavier sisters in Christ feel when they see me showing off my narrow waistline? Exactly *who* is being edified by my attire?"

Ouch. These were tough questions to ask, and even tougher to answer. Still, I needed to adjust my dress because, though my clothes weren't tight or necessarily immodest in and of themselves, the issue was the motivation of my heart – my intentions. When I faced the naked facts, I understood why I chose clothes that highlighted my narrow waistline and slender frame. I discovered I was vain. And I concluded that vanity is pride and pride is sin. I faced the fact that I chose my clothes based on a certain level of pride, and that I was more interested in my own glory than in God's. What a wake-up call this was for a woman who considered herself to be a faithful follower of Christ for twenty years!

So how could I have been living this way for twenty years and been so blind? Well, I think there are a couple of reasons for this. For one, I was foolish – plain and simple. I take full responsibility for my sin and I am grieved by it.

Secondly, I wanted to be accepted. I wanted to fit in. In truth, I really just wanted to be loved. But to be loved and accepted by people in the current American culture (and sadly, sometimes in today's church culture, as well) I felt I had to hold to their standards of beauty and attire. Show a little more skin. Skip a few meals to be thinner. And if I hold to the standards of the current culture, I am bound by those standards. And if I am bound by those standards, I am imprisoned by those standards. And if imprisoned, then I am finally consumed by those standards. It's as though there is no way out, and I feel I am on an endless quest to have more, to be thinner, to be prettier, to somehow out-do the next woman. It is a never ending cycle and it is absolutely, unequivocally exhausting.

I think of the apostle Paul, who cries out in Romans 7:24-25: *What a wretched man I am! Who will rescue me from this body of death? Thanks be to God – through Jesus Christ our Lord!*

God was showing up to rescue me. I just knew it. And, oh, how I needed rescuing! No, I didn't want to be seen as weird or some sort of Christian oddball, but I really wanted out of the rat race that this elusive dream of physical beauty had now become for me. Covering as an outward sign of my devotion to God and as a sign of my submission to my husband's authority were tremendously important to me, and were the main reasons I chose to cover. But I also clearly understood that God was offering me a way to "opt out" of the frenzy of trying to constantly keep up with the world's standard of beauty. I didn't have to subscribe to its code any longer. Now I could finally move from the 'head' knowledge of knowing what the Bible said about true and lasting beauty to actually *living out* what I said I believed. Somehow, before, I felt unable to do that. There is no doubt that I felt this was God's way of answering my (desperate) prayers over my distorted body image.

The Big Cover Up

My husband liked the way I wore my head wraps, but now my covering had taken on a whole new meaning altogether. But I admit I was slow in telling him that I had made up my mind and decided to commit to covering. It just sort of hung out there in space until he brought it up a couple of weeks after I'd made the commitment. I just knew he would not be thrilled about it and, I confess, I avoided having the conversation. But then when he finally brought it up, there was not much of a conversation to have, as he seemed fairly accepting of it. Still, something unspoken seemed to hang in the air. It was bound to expose itself, and one day it did.

"What? What *is* it?" I asked him one evening, noticing a somewhat disagreeable look on his face as we talked.

"I don't know," he started.

"Go on, tell me," I said slowly, in a calm and even tone. This was our way of gently urging the other to speak his or her heart. We had this technique down well after fifteen years of marriage.

"I don't know. I'm just not feeling the head wraps anymore," he began. "It's getting sort of old."

My heart sank, but I tried to remain upbeat. "Okay," I said, trying to hide my hurt feelings.

"Do you want me to try new ways of wearing it?" I'd tried some various ways of wearing the cloth on my head, but it usually ended up in a Nubian-style wrap because it was easiest and quickest. Plus, I just really liked the way it looked.

"No, not really. It doesn't really matter how you wear it. I just don't like your head covered. I find you more attractive with no covering at all."

"Oh. Okay." I really didn't know what to say. But clearly I had overestimated his acceptance of my head covering. I told him I appreciated his honesty – and I did. I really wanted to know how he felt on the matter. But it still hurt. It really hurt.

Later I gave him some information I'd found with reasons, myths and further biblical explanations on head covering. He stuck it in his Bible, and I hoped he would get around to reading it. But I wasn't sure. He told me he'd been praying about it, but really had not felt God speaking anything in particular to him about it. Later on he told me that he could see from the I Corinthians passage that it was perfectly acceptable to cover during church worship. This freed me to cover on Sundays, and I was simply delighted.

Balancing Act

Before this defining conversation with my husband, I had been covering my head almost all the time. For me, it seemed nearly impossible to separate praying with my head covered (considering the directives of I Corinthians 11:1-16) from living my normal, day-to-day life. I was *always* praying, always talking to God about this little thing or that big thing. I lived my whole life as a prayer. So for me, keeping my head covered all the time just made sense. But now, things would have to change.

Right after my last conversation with my husband, I began to cover my head only part of the time. He didn't much care if I covered while he was gone or at work. So I began to cover most of the day at home and whenever I was out in public without him. After praying with the children and putting them to bed at night, I would take off my covering. This way he would see my hair when he returned from work. This had been going well for quite a while, until one day he let me know that he felt he was taking a back seat to head covering. He felt that it was a decision that affected only me, and that it had very little to do with *him*. I felt hurt. And misunderstood. And I'd be lying if I said I didn't think his comments reeked of selfishness. I really wanted him (and others in my life) to see my covering as an act of obedience, not just something I adopted for my own fun and pleasure. Not that any of this was much fun anyway! In my hurt I wondered what the purpose was in covering if it didn't make a difference in areas of my life that really meant the most – like my relationship with my husband. I felt so discouraged that I wanted to forget about head covering and give it up altogether. It was, after all, such a *small* thing. Did it really make that much difference, anyway? I think any woman with any interest in covering has to come to the point where she asks herself how important this thing is to her. And only she can answer that question.

Later, I told my husband how much I appreciated his honesty. And I really did. Sure, it hurt, but at least I was aware of the fact that I needed to change some things. I began to see past the smoke screen of his comments and discern what his real needs were: he didn't want to play second fiddle to my new passion. I began to reorder my priorities so that the spirituality of my covering expressed itself in increased and sincere devotion to my husband. He noticed almost immediately, and then seemed to endlessly sing my praises! We soon found renewed intimacy in our marriage. Once I began to consider his needs more, he was visibly happier. And this made me happier. He needed to feel important and not outdone by head covering. Once I truly understood that, I became much more at peace about covering. I still uncover my head when he's home. And sometimes he might not even mind if I'm covered in his presence, so long as I don't overdo it. When I told him I was writing this book, he told me that he was proud of me, and he encouraged me every step of the way as I wrote about covering. Finding the right balance with my husband was key. Married women who desire to cover their heads must seek to find a harmonious balance, as well, if that is at all possible.

An Open Door

Not long after I began covering, a dear friend sent me an email telling me how much she supports my head covering. She said that though head covering seems to cause other women to feel in bondage, it seems to have had the exact opposite effect on me. She knows me well. She also said she didn't want me to think she didn't care because we'd not had a lengthy discussion about covering. I told her it was fine, and that it's just not my mode of operation to bash my friends over the head with a book on covering. Some women have had really sweeping transformations with regard to covering and dressing more modestly. But for me, I told my friend, it was as if God was opening a door. I could either walk through that door, or I could walk away from the door. If I walked away from the door I already knew what would await me: self-doubt, bondage, anxiety, pride, vanity and continuing issues with body image.

If, however, I walked through the door that He was opening, I had a real chance at peace and freedom. I would be free to define my beauty by God's standards. I could exchange my pride and vanity for humility, wisdom and purity. I could tune out the noise of the world's lies and step into real truth. It was just a door, and the choice was mine.

I like to think I made the right choice by walking through that door. Maybe it's different for other women. Maybe it's less of an open door and more of a command. Or maybe it's less of a command and more of a whisper. After I made the decision to cover, everything didn't just magically fall into place. I still struggled with things like doubt and the perceptions of others. But I felt I was on the right track. And if I was struggling, at least I was struggling in the right direction.

*C*hapter 3

Joanna's Pearl

*Again, the kingdom of heaven is like a merchant
looking for fine pearls. When he found one of
great value, he went away and sold everything
he had and bought it.* – Matthew 13:45-46

"Why is it when I wore my jeans and shirts too
tight, or ran around the beach in a bikini no
Christian felt it necessary to say anything to me
about it? Why did *that* not raise concern for my
Christian testimony? Yet when I wear very
modest attire and choose to cover my head
Christians become uncomfortable and concerned
for me spiritually."

With a desire to grow closer to Christ, Joanna,
a homemaker, wife and mother of three, asked
God to open her eyes to anything that might be
keeping her from making Jesus her all. She
wanted Him to be the costly Pearl that would be
the single most important thing in her life, and
she wanted to see her sins for what they were.
She wanted Christ to make her aware of any
worldly thinking she had, or lies she might have
mistaken for truth. And then she waited. It wasn't
long before she felt God responding.

"I soon felt a sense of grief and a desire to
repent over my short hair," she says. "I started
looking into Scripture for the reason why my
spirit was so grieved. That's when I read I
Corinthians 11:1-16. From this passage, it seemed
very clear to me that a woman's head being
covered was of significance. To me, it seemed less
of a custom and more of a command that was to
be obeyed."

For Joanna, reading this passage of Scripture marked the beginning of a meaningful, emotional and ultimately fleeting, journey. Head covering seemed such a weighty matter, yet Joanna was left wondering why she'd never heard any pastor preach on the topic, nor had she known any Christian to talk about it.

Still, Joanna couldn't let go of the idea of covering her head. She spent weeks praying and reading the I Corinthians passage again and again. She read articles on head covering and learned the original Greek words used in the I Corinthians passage. In the end, she couldn't ignore her deep desire to honor the command, so she talked to her husband about it.

"He was more than a little taken back by the idea," she says. Still, she asked him to read the passage and to pray about it. She also offered him various articles on head covering to read. "I understand why it took him by surprise," she says. "Like me, he had never heard anyone preach on its relevance for today."

Despite Joanna's longing to be obedient and cover her head, she also wanted to honor her husband and his feelings. He neither understood nor was comfortable with the idea of Joanna wearing a head covering. "In the beginning, I know I exasperated him greatly," she says. "I wanted him to give me his wondrous blessing and to tell me how proud he was of me for going against the grain in order to be obedient to God." That wondrous blessing never came. But he eventually resigned, telling Joanna that if covering meant that much to her, she should go ahead and do it. She was thrilled. It wasn't the blessing she had hoped for, but she rejoiced, anyway. "I love my husband dearly," she says. "I appreciate him loving me even when he is at a loss to understand me!"

Strength in Numbers

Joanna began her covering journey with the same enthusiasm common with many women who are new to covering their heads. She started a blog and soon found an online support system that was comprised of many other head covering women. "When God first put it on my heart to cover my head it took great courage to be obedient! There was no one around me, in my family or church, who could relate to what God had put on my heart. It was incredibly uplifting when God brought encouragement and support to me from readers of my blog," she says. "Christian women who could actually relate to me were praying for me," she shares excitedly. "How humbling and special that was to me. I needed them right then."

From the enthusiastic response to her blog, Joanna suspected that God was up to something. She encouraged the readers of her blog to press on to be faithful to God, even if they felt alone in their desire to cover. "Through the blog alone it became very apparent to me that God was stirring the hearts of many Christian women throughout the Unites States to cover their heads," Johanna relates. She began to offer prayer support to other women online who, like her, had a deep desire to cover.

But soon it became apparent that Joanna was as much in need of prayer as any of the women she encouraged through her blog. It became clearer to her that though she had received her husband's very apathetic consent, she never obtained his true blessing. She realized her mistake.

"The problem was that it wasn't something I'd given him time to pray about or come to peace about. I simply made my passionate plea with persistence to the point that he gave in!" she says. She realized that the prodding her eager resolve produced wasn't fair to her husband. "That was simply sugar-coated manipulation," she now admits.

Joanna now had to reexamine her decision to cover. In an effort to follow Christ completely, she had bypassed her husband's position of authority, something that was contrary to the teaching of the I Corinthians passage that had come to mean so much to her. "My husband is over me," she says. "He is to be the spiritual leader. When God put it on my heart to cover my head, I should have presented my convictions to my husband and then allowed him time to pray about it and come to the decision that he was to come to. Even if he had said 'no', I could have rested in knowing that the Lord knew my heart and my desire to obey. God would not have faulted me; my husband is to be the leader and he is accountable to the Lord for the final decision."

Joanna and her husband agreed to approach the head covering decision again through prayer. They agreed to pray together each night, for one week. This time, though, the spiritual reins would be in her husband's hands. They both agreed that whatever her husband's final decision, Joanna would accept. They came to this conclusion after some emotionally tense conversations. Despite the fact that she was now facing the possibility that her husband might not let her continue to cover, there was now a new intimacy between her and her husband. "God used those very emotional conversations to knit our hearts together more closely than ever before," she says. "We were both seeking the Lord's direction together on all things, at a level we never had before."

For the time being, both Joanna and her husband agreed that she would continue to cover. "I am thankful that my husband believed that God put it on my heart to cover my head. He said that just as I should not have rushed into something of this magnitude, it would also be a mistake for him to rashly make a decision for me to stop wearing it. I appreciated the wisdom in that," she says. Continuing on in her head covering journey, Joanna was met with the challenges of head covering outside of the home – dealing with the reactions of extended family members, church members and friends. Although those times weren't easy, Joanna never doubted the value in head covering, nor did she doubt that God was calling her to it. But there was also the pain of being misunderstood, dejected and alone. She wondered if her husband felt embarrassed by her. She wondered if her family believed in her convictions. Her prayers were mingled with tears. "I will fully admit, I cried a lot," she says. "But it made me realize how much I have looked to others for their affirmation. Being obedient to what God asked of me made me different. And being different was difficult for me." She recalled the initial prayer that led to her head covering. "I remember I asked that I would find my identity in Jesus alone. In sensing that others were questioning me instead of admiring me, I had to rely fully on the Lord; I had to cry out to Him for strength and peace. I had to lean wholly on Him and find my identity in Him."

A Prophet without Honor

Joanna's decision to cover was met with the most disdain from, oddly enough, other Christians. "Christians say we should be cultural, but what does that mean? Does that mean we align ourselves with the standards of the world in order to fit in? The world doesn't base its choices on God's standards," she says. "The world bases its choices and actions on the flesh and on self-promotion." Joanna struggled to understand how looking like everybody else should better equip Christians to impact the world for Christ. "It just doesn't make sense to me," she says. "I think the world has lost a lot of interest in Christianity because the differences between us and the world are so few; they think we are hypocrites. Have people lost hope in Christianity because we give them nothing to set us apart?" Joanna remembers the deep and lasting impact of her grandmother's Christian witness. "She was not like the world around her. She always wore dresses, always had her hair up in a bun and never wore makeup. People did notice she was different in her appearance. Was her testimony hurt because she was not 'cultural', appearing like the world around her? No. She remains one of the most respected women I know."

Joanna isn't reluctant about admitting the role that she thinks fear plays in the lives of many Christians. "Why do some Christians think that having a different standard than the world will scare unbelievers away? I don't think it would scare unbelievers away. I think it would intrigue them. They would watch me to see what makes me choose a different standard. I don't think they are scared," she says. "I think it's Christians who are scared. Why are we afraid to be marked as a believer? It saddens me that by no longer desiring to fit in with the world, I am also no longer fitting in with most Christian circles."

The Beginning of the End

It was a cold and blustery day in Northern Indiana when Joanna sat at her computer. She rested her face in her hands. She was thankful – so thankful – for having connected with so many people who cared about her journey. Those who encouraged her and validated her feelings made her often misunderstood covering journey more bearable. She had gained so much comfort from other women who loved Christ with the same passion that she did. Some questioned and disagreed; others listened and even cried for her. But always there were the prayers of dear sisters who cared for her and her covering journey. But now it was time to tell them. With a heavy sigh, but a confident heart, Joanna sat up straight in her chair and placed her fingers on the keyboard. She typed slowly at first, but soon she was typing more vigorously, her fingers infused with the same passion for God that got her started on this uncertain journey.

"I was hopeful that God would give a divine revelation to my husband. You know, something like some disturbing nightmare where he would see demons chasing me and they would be unable to touch me because I was marked," she quipped. "Although that would have been a good story, that's not the way God worked."

It was Wednesday morning. It started the same as many other mornings, except that Joanna felt an odd sense of great peace. After washing and blow drying her hair, she didn't feel the same urge to cover her head. She did wear her head covering that day, but she felt that God might be preparing her for her husband's refusal of the covering. "I just had a sense that the decision had been made. I sensed the answer was a 'no' and that was okay. Now, anyone who has followed my journey knows it is with passion and courage I have covered my head, so I knew it was the Holy Spirit who was allowing me that peace that passes understanding."

The next day her husband gave his answer. "With loving tears he said he was sorry," she says. "He had prayed about it, but he hadn't felt any change of conviction on the issue. He was very affirming in his love for me and he was concerned about hurting me."

Joanna knew that the decision would sadden many of her readers. With zealous fingers she typed her blog post, assuring her faithful readers that she was doing well and not in turmoil over the decision. She felt blessed, loved and deeply cared for by God. God had not forsaken her. Indeed, He knew the heart of His beloved Joanna, and He answered her prayer during the course of her emotional, three week head covering journey.

"My initial plea was that I would find my identity in Christ alone and not be focused on what others thought of me. I wanted not to be concerned with the affirmation of others, but willing to do anything the Lord wanted me to," she says. "Well, I certainly never entertained the idea that He would put those covering convictions on my heart in order to do that! It blows me away how He so cleverly and perfectly answered my prayer through a three week journey. All I had to go on for those three weeks was the trust that I'd placed in what God had spoken to my heart. I clung to Jesus, delighted in Him, and found my identity in Him alone. He gave me the courage to be obedient and faithful, to do what He had asked of me in the face of great opposition. The Lord knows it was a spiritual victory!"

Instead of causing division, Joanna believes the head covering issue actually deepened the intimacy between her and her husband. They prayed together more. They enjoyed more meaningful conversations. Though it was emotionally risky, they exposed themselves more. But in the end, their marriage was stronger and better than ever.

Though her head covering journey was a short-lived one, Joanna admits she misses covering. "In its absence, I've realized how much the physical sign of the head covering helped me focus on honoring the Lord," she says. "The head covering material did not have any power in itself; but what it represented in my heart was powerful. Each time I put my covering on I prayed that I would bring honor to the Lord in being marked as His child. Each time I looked in the mirror and saw the covering, it prompted humility in me."

No longer covering her head has not diminished Joanna's desire to remain humble and gentle in spirit. "I know it comes from the heart," she says. "I am the same daughter of the King without a cloth on my head. To some who don't know my heart and the details of my journey, it may seem I am a confused soul, but I know I have found my identity in my Lord Jesus. Still," she continues, "The head covering journey has been a blessing, and I will always be a head covering lady at heart."

Chapter 4

A Visible Sign

Have nothing to do with the fruitless deeds of darkness, but rather expose them... everything exposed by the light becomes visible, for it is light that makes everything visible. – Ephesians 5:11, 13-14a

"I lost my faith in religion early on – way before I actually abandoned it."

Amber, a 26-year-old single woman, briefly spent time as an atheist, an agnostic, and a much longer time as a witch. "I grew up in an extremely abusive household," she says. "My mother married my adoptive father when I was about four. He was an alcoholic and a drug addict, though initially he was a nice and charming man – a step up from my biological father." Much of Amber's childhood was spent in fear and anger. "In the house I grew up in," she tells, "women were weak and useless. I didn't want to be a woman. We lived in fear, and the men had all the power. The end result was that I grew up hating myself in some twisted fashion, and even after we no longer lived in that house, I just knew that being a woman was some horrible flaw," she says. "I had a lot of anger. It drove me away from men and it drove me away from religion, because it was obviously something invented by men to lord over women in order to hold us down. I'd worked through most of these issues by the time I embraced religion again, but it wasn't a sudden change. It all happened pretty gradually."

Despite the fact that Amber was raised Missouri Synod Lutheran (a high church form of Lutheranism), she admits that for most of her life she was a Christian in name only. Her family did not discuss religion, so her doubts and questions about religion went unaddressed for a long time. Things began to change, though, when Amber's mother divorced and later married a man who was reformed Mennonite. Amber later moved in with her mother, her new stepfather and his parents. "All of them were more religious than I was," she says. "To be perfectly honest, I held all faiths in general contempt. I went through the motions, but I didn't believe they did any good – merely that they focused my intentions and my will toward a good goal."

Amber felt more comfortable discussing religion with her stepfather than with anyone else in her family. Though initially those discussions were shallow, Amber finally entertained the possibility of having some of her questions answered, and she was posing more of them all the time.

Searching for God

"I finally decided, one night, to just ask," she says. "I literally asked God to 'prove it' – prove to me that He existed, and that I should bother obeying Him. I went to bed that night questioning," she says, "and woke up the next morning knowing that it was true. From there, it became a question of which faith to follow." Amber was drawn to the standard of modesty required of Muslim women, and felt especially drawn to the hijab, the head covering typically worn by Muslim women. "And really," she now admits, "that's not a good reason to choose a faith, so I moved on." Trying to push the idea of head covering out of her mind, Amber went about visiting different churches, trying to find a place to call home. She was so moved by a Catholic Mass she attended, that she immediately went out and bought a Catholic Bible and began to read. "I found Catholic message boards online and began to peruse them. Over time, I decided to convert to Catholicism. After I made the decision to convert, I came across a discussion on a Catholic message board about the use of mantillas in the Latin Mass. The feeling I got at that moment was like being punched in the chest," she says. "It was, literally, a physical sensation. I felt God was saying 'Do this!' but I resisted. I told myself that it was an old-fashioned tradition, that it was no longer a requirement and that I didn't need to wear a covering. I told myself that most women don't wear them, anyway, and that I would just look silly.

"But the thought just wouldn't leave me alone," Amber continues, "so I started investigating." Amber explored sites and blogs where Muslim women gave their reasons for covering. "They said they were doing it not because they were forced, but because God had commanded it. They would then list the reasons behind the command, but it came down to something as simple as that. God said so."

Amber continued to search the internet, finding arguments both for and against covering in worship. "I went looking for more arguments in favor of the continued covering by women in their churches," she says. "Boy, did I ever find them! I found some wonderful, well thought out, well researched posts and articles. There was this entire community of women out there who felt as I was beginning to feel – that God had called them to this, to covering."

Small Beginnings
Amber found the argument in support of covering to be compelling, and she wanted to

begin somewhere. "I wanted to start covering in a subtle way, so as not to distract the other parishioners from their worship. I was distracting enough, since I wasn't able to take communion yet, and so I started wearing large headbands," she says. "But I felt, at least for me, that this was cheating. It didn't cover my head, not at all. But for the time being, it was what I had. While I tried to work out what to do, the headbands were better than nothing."

In the midst of Amber's issues about her headbands, she was struck by another thought. "Suddenly, it comes to me that we are also instructed to pray unceasingly. So, I think 'Right. I can do that. Oh! But wait, I have to cover when I pray!' So I borrowed a scarf from one of my sisters – this ugly, purple and green polka dot thing – and used it to cover while I prayed at home. Then one day, doing yard work, enjoying the sun and the weather and trimming our trees, the thought came to me: I am constantly surrounded by God and His angels. If He is everywhere, and we are to cover in His Presence, then that means covering all the time. Everywhere. And it was that simple. I would cover all the time," she says. "When I became convinced that I needed to cover all the time, I ordered two snoods, one in black and one in white." Amber freely admits that she was still apprehensive about covering; even when she felt convinced it was something she should do. Buying only two snoods meant a minimal financial investment for her. "You see, I was still nervous, still worried that I would feel like an idiot, or that people would say something." Later, Amber would grow more comfortable with covering, and would eventually branch out to wearing shawls, tiechels and even hijab; though she says she doesn't wear the hijab in the traditional Muslim fashion.

Amber soon told her family that she had made the decision to cover, and she explained to them her reasons why. "My mother, while she doesn't agree with my belief about head covering, accepts it," she says. "She only has two complaints. One, in her words, 'You have beautiful hair, and it's a shame to keep it covered'. And two, she's afraid that, given the political climate and the occasional ignorance of people, someone will mistake me for a Muslim and harass me or hurt me. My stepfather shares her concern for my safety. He, like my mother, doesn't agree with me, but he believes that it's my choice."

Amber says that her friends have been fairly easygoing about her choice to cover. "They all sort of shrug," she says. "My friends don't consider religion a factor in our friendship, so they just view it as an odd fashion choice. One of my friends jokes that I don't really 'like' it, but that I've just gotten used to it, which is why I won't take it off like a normal person. My best friend, while she doesn't really understand, is supportive, and helps me to find modest clothes on sale, because she knows that I hate to shop."

A Shift in Perspectives

Amber is conscious of the ways that covering has affected some of her negative attitudes about men. "I'm adversarial with men on many levels," she says, "and I'm not nearly as respectful as I should be to men who deserve my respect, like my stepfather. But things are different now. I still have some negative thoughts about men, but not as many," she says. Despite the scars that have shaped her attitudes about men in authority, Amber notices how her attitude toward her stepfather is changing and improving. "If we are having a discussion and there becomes a point we disagree on, I stop to think, I pause, I take a second, and I remember that he is a good man, with many years of experience on me, and I think about what he is saying. And you know, he's not always right. But I can have a conversation with him, and we can work to a solution. In the past, he was always willing to do this, but I wasn't," she admits. "The covering makes me more careful about how I speak to others, what I think."

If covering has made Amber more aware of her attitudes towards men, it has also made her more aware of her identity as a woman – something that her shattered past tempted her to deny. "I'm moving, not just to cover, but to dress more modestly, to embrace my femininity," she says. "I cover, and I know that in my heart, this means that I am embracing a countercultural point of view. I believe, in my heart, even though I don't always manage to show it yet, that there is an order to the world, instituted by God, and that everyone has a place in it. The differences between men and women exist for a reason, and we both have our roles to play. Despite what the world wants us to think, one is not better than the other; rather, the roles complement each other: where one is weak, the other is strong. And there's no shame in that, no reason to fight and degrade one another.

"I cover, and it makes me hesitate to give into my first rude impulse. I cover and it reminds me to follow God's Law. It reminds me to love others, to treat them as I would want them to treat me, even when they are treating me badly," she says. "It reminds me that, lacking a husband, the authority in our house belongs to my Dad, so even when I don't want to get up off my butt and help when he asks, I should, because he does deserve my respect. He's not unreasonable; he loves my mother, my sister and me, and he is doing his best to lead our family and keep us happy and comfortable and together. I cover and it reminds me that when someone forgets to put their dishes away, it's not some subtle inference that I'm the maid. It's just a sign that they're human, too, and that they forgot to pick up their coffee mug. I cover and it is a physical reminder that I am always surrounded by God and the angels, and while they know what I do, even in secret, I want to do things God's way – even when that's not my first impulse.

"I still have my anger," Amber shares honestly. "My temper is not something that I'm proud of. The urge to rip into people who aren't doing things the way I think they should be done hasn't magically dissipated. I have the vocabulary of a sailor, and I can curse in five languages, four of which I can't say anything polite in," she quips. "But the covering makes me hesitate. It's a visible sign of an invisible change, a charge that I have willingly taken upon myself."

Chapter 5

Black and Plain

Do not conform any longer to the pattern of this world, but be transformed by the renewing of your mind. Then you will be able to test and approve what God's will is – his good, pleasing and perfect will. – Romans 12:2

In all the stories we've read about the Amish or Conservative Mennonites, in all the pictures we've seen, we sense a peaceful, simple existence that the more quiet parts of us long for. Maybe we wouldn't admit it. And perhaps we are only romanticizing about a way of existence that is far, far beyond the reach of our ordinary, often frenetic and harried lives. Still, we imagine ourselves, even if for a moment, living in such a world. What would it be like? We've seen pictures of the women: their faces without makeup, their hair covered, their dresses long, their arduous work full of purpose, often reflected in the strength of their hands. In the pictures that we see of such women, they are all, well...*White*. It's easy to imagine ourselves in a world where everyone looks like we do – even if that world is much different from the one we live in every day. But what if we were a racial minority? What if the color of our skin changed the landscape of our imaginings?

Although I am not plain, there have certainly been times when I have felt like the only head covering Black woman with Anabaptist tendencies in my entire corner of the world. But that was before Regina. You might imagine my shock when she visited my blog and commented

41

that she was an African-American head covering plain woman. I had to know more.

Little Girl Lost

It isn't with fondness that Regina, 48, recalls her childhood. She admits that it wasn't a happy time. "My parents fought and my dad drank," she says. "He did finally get saved when I was in my 20s, but he had a heart attack in 1984 and passed away. I was just twenty-three at the time. I had only been a Christian myself for a couple of years." A shy child, Regina says she didn't always fit in at school and was often teased for no reason. Though she wasn't seeking to garner attention, she eventually had to deal with the stares that at times still prove challenging. For starters, Regina fell in love with and married a White man. "Tim and I met at the church he was going to, and I thought he was kind of cute," she recalls, fondly. "Our first date was a baptism at his church. I needed a ride to the church, and someone asked him if he would give me a ride," she says. "I was told I had a ride, but that I needed to wear jeans. I thought this was weird because it was nearly one hundred degrees outside, but I thought maybe the church had a rule against shorts. Imagine my surprise when Tim shows up on his motorcycle! He rode a motorcycle because he didn't have a car that ran. Anyway, the rest is history," she says. Regina and Tim have three daughters who round out their happy family. When asked about the difficulties that many interracial couples face, Regina notes that their marital journey has been a good one. "We haven't had any real challenges except the occasional stare," she says. "Now that I dress the way I do, we *really* get stares!"

Let Her Be...*Curious*

As with many women who cover, Regina came upon the idea of covering quite by accident. "In May of 2005 I was online, and while I was looking for something else, I came across a site where I found an internet version of ""...Let Her Be Veiled."", by Tom Shank. I read it all the way through," she says. "The author wrote about why women are to wear a head covering and he talked in great detail about I Corinthians 11:1-16," she remembers. "After reading it through, I sent the link to a Christian online group I belonged to, and I asked members there what they thought. They all thought the author was way off base and was twisting the Scriptures." But Regina suspected there was something more that had yet to be discovered. "After reading their responses, I still wasn't really satisfied, but I decided to put the whole issue on the backburner for a while."

Regina went the remainder of spring and most of that summer not giving much attention to the covering idea. But by the end of summer, things began to change. "In August someone had posted something to the same Christian online group I was a member of," she says. "A woman was doing a Bible study on women's head covering and needed information. I didn't respond to her post, but others did," she remembers. "They were against the head covering. Someone even posted something by a woman preacher who claimed that women ought not to wear a covering. I can't clearly recall the preacher's reasons, though," she says, "something about how it's important not to appear 'holier than thou', or something to this effect.

"The day I read this woman's post, I was leaving to go to a Christian family retreat, and there was to be a woman there whom I remembered as a head covering Christian," she says. "I had made up my mind to ask her about it while we were at the retreat.

"After dinner one evening, I finally asked her about her 'head covering thingie', as I called it then. In my mind, I was thinking, 'Please don't say anything about I Corinthians 11'. But of course, she told me that her covering was out of obedience to I Corinthians 11:1-16. In my head I was thinking, 'You just *had* to say it!'" Regina says, humorously. "She went on to tell me that at first, her husband didn't want her to wear the covering; but after careful study, they both knew it was the right thing to do," she says. "But what was really amazing was that her 14-year-old daughter was the first to even suggest head covering!"

A Reason to Believe

This time, Regina chose not to put the head covering idea on the back burner. She was hungering for real truth. "Later on that night at the retreat, I got settled in our cabin and I got out my Bible. I really read I Corinthians 11:1-16 and I underlined it. I read this passage for the next several days, and the more I read and prayed, the more I felt that God wanted me to cover," she says. "But at first, I was a bit annoyed at (the apostle) Paul for not making these verses clear to me," she jests. "I soon joined another Christian online group, but this one was for Christians who cover," she says, "and that was really helpful."

For many women who feel led of God to cover their heads, telling their husbands about their feelings is often the proverbial 'moment of truth'. As they seek to please and honor God by seeking to honor their husbands, these women often feel that their husband's response could either validate or discourage covering in the future. "I finally asked my husband Tim about it," Regina says, "and he wasn't sure about it, but he said 'If that is what God is telling you to do, then you need to obey Him.' He also wanted to study the I Corinthians passage. I had also received a printed copy of ""...Let Her Be Veiled."" and Tim read it from cover to cover," she says. "He was surprised and very glad that I wanted to obey these verses. So, I have been covering since September of 2005."

Regina says Tim is still supportive of her covering and recognizes ways that covering has changed her. "I'm more submissive than I used to be," she says. "I'm not saying our marriage is perfect, but I find I'm more respectful of Tim and more willing to submit to his authority. I was always a submissive wife and respected Tim greatly, but the 'thing on my head' is a constant reminder of my willingness to obey the Lord and to honor my husband."

Regina isn't especially close to her blood relatives who live far away, so their opinions of her covering don't affect her. The response of her friends, however, has been mixed. "My friends haven't treated me any differently, but some have responded with questions and curiosity," she says, "and some think I'm legalistic. A lot of people I know don't even ask me about my covering." Regina is not a part of a head covering church, though she would like to be. "Both Tim and I believe God has us in our current church for a reason," she says. "We don't want to leave, but it would be nice to worship with like-minded people. I'm hoping that sometime in the future God will lead us to a conservative Mennonite church. We have seen the worldliness in many churches and we are both saddened by this. Of course, the Mennonite church is not perfect, but we were pleased by their unwillingness to conform to the world in many areas, including their response to head covering." Though of great importance to her, Regina recognizes that covering is just one aspect of a life of holiness lived for God. "Wearing a covering isn't a salvation issue, but an obedience issue," she maintains. "Wearing a covering isn't going to get you into Heaven."

For Regina, who keeps her head covered at all times, dressing modestly was a natural by-product of covering. "I wear jumpers and cape dresses every day; a cape dress is a long dress with an extra bodice in the front and back to conceal the upper form," she explains. "I feel more feminine and Tim really likes me in dresses, too. I wanted to be plain because I was sick of trying to keep up with the latest fashion trends. But that doesn't mean I wear potato sacks in black all the time," she concedes. "Cape dresses are very pretty and feminine and can be made in a variety of colors and styles. It's not always easy to dress this way, though. But I do have support from my plain friends in the conservative Mennonite churches." In addition to her plain friends, Regina says her greatest support network is comprised of her husband, children and Christian online groups that advocate head covering.

Chapter 6

One Small Obedient Thing

As the body without the spirit is dead, so faith without deeds is dead. – James 2:26

Lisa is a 41-year-old married mother of four, who has covered for about two years. Lisa's website, *Those Head Coverings*, is a blog whose purpose is to offer head covering resources, news items of interest and general encouragement for women who are interested in covering. Lisa's website was one of the first I encountered as I struggled to come to terms with the idea of covering. I found links to meaningful articles, the websites of other covering women and the place where I first encountered a richer understanding of head covering and, equally as important, a real sense of *community* – there were really other women like me out there; I was not alone. Lisa's blog proves to be a hub of activity – connecting women who cover, offering spiritual insights and being an ongoing presence of encouragement and light when "small" matters like head covering are often easily dismissed, even at times by the Christian community.

"I truly hope to encourage others by making them aware of the simple, quiet blogs where women have written about the reasons they choose to cover, their difficulties and their joys as they embark upon a change of lifestyle, and sometimes I might share the ways that women are wearing their head coverings," she says. "They have all encouraged me – from the young women who began covering in a place where no one else did, to the women who grew up in communities where everyone covered. In this simple act of obedience," she says, "we can be won over to a humble, honorable and beautiful way of life."

Easy Assumptions

Lisa was raised attending church regularly, but she began to really take her faith seriously during her college years. A family friend gave Lisa a book called "The Head Coverings of I Corinthians 11", by Paul K. Williams. "I had read verses 1-16 of that chapter before and assumed it was all spiritual," she says, "and that nothing physical was meant, and I just glossed over it. I was remaining so steadfast in the 'we are all equal in God's eyes' stance, that I actually overlooked the differences in men and women's roles while here on earth. When I began to study this passage in depth, and was more ready and able to grasp the idea that men and women are made for different reasons, for different purposes, and that the head covering is a symbol and reminder of these things, it became a real eye-opener for grasping more of the blessings that God has for women of God, and the invisible, patient, trusting and submissive strength that we really have."

Lisa says that her husband felt that her decision to cover was her personal choice, but he did also read the book by Williams. They also both read "Glories Seen and Unseen", by Warren Henderson. "My husband is sort of ambivalent about it, still; though in the beginning, he reminded me more, and helped me make time to go out and find something to put on, when I didn't have anything but a couple of hats," she says. "Though he does not feel that head covering is a requirement, he feels that if a woman chooses to cover, it is a good thing and that she should not be discouraged from it." How has her head covering affected her children? "My daughter, who is eleven, used to always want to wear a scarf, too, to be like Mom, but she doesn't always anymore," Lisa says. "My older son, who is 12, has asked me about it, and when I read the passage of Scripture to him and asked him what he thought, he said it made sense that I should cover."

Experimenting with Styles

The fact that Lisa is not a part of a head covering church or denomination doesn't seem to slow her down. "We try to be less traditional- or denomination-minded and just more Bible following." So what are some challenges faced by this grounded, articulate and confident woman of God? "Finding a style, for one," she offers. "Hats are socially acceptable sometimes, but not always quite reverent enough at other times. A head scarf wrap makes folks wonder why you're wearing a Muslim head covering. A plain white head scarf has made a few people jokingly ask about my Amish leanings. I still switch around and play with styles." Lisa overcomes this challenge by looking online to find out how other women are wearing their coverings. "I keep my eyes open for the more stylish looks, so that I'm not copying someone's 'religious' style, if that makes sense," she says.

Finding Beauty in Faith

Lisa says that one of her greatest joys in covering is seeing how it affects her outward behavior, as well as how people see her. "I'm amazed at how a piece of cloth – whether on my head or in my style of clothes – can affect my own attitude, as well as how I am treated by others," she says. "My respect for God's words and for my husband has shifted to something more spiritual – which is odd to me, considering that it's a physical thing that brings about this spiritual awareness. I do feel pretty and feminine too, and that helps me feel more peaceful with myself somehow."

Along her covering journey, Lisa has learned about other covering women for whom she has gained a deep respect, and through whom she has gained a greater appreciation for the truth, values and beauty of her faith. "I have been very encouraged since I got more involved in reading and researching online," she says. "I have found ladies of all sorts who want to dress more modestly, but feel that they are alone in their region, city, church, temple, mosque, clique, school or workplace. I have found ladies of all sorts who desire – intelligently – to cover their heads, to be at home and to rear up their own children and to joyfully submit to a spiritually-minded man. It makes me more and more certain that there really is one substantial Truth to the old-fashioned values of home, family, femininity, motherhood, purity and spirituality," she says. "Some of us were reared up in a culture or home or tradition that excluded our ability to find the whole Truth, but we stayed faithful to the Truth that we were seeking. Some of the ladies I have found online and in books had to really leave their father and mother, their homeland and the religious background which they grew up adhering to. They never left their searching – and finding – of Truth."

Though others might see Lisa's distinguished presence in the blogosphere as a needed and much appreciated source of encouragement and support, she admits that she's been as much a recipient as a giver of encouragement for head covering women. "I have found most of my support and encouragement online," she says. "It's there that I've found public testimonies of faithful obedience and the examples of lives that have been touched by wearing a little piece of cloth. Even if I've never met these women who in strength chose to do something different from others because of their own convictions and understanding of Scripture – even if I don't know them, even if we don't understand worship, or church or even God the same way – I may be one of few who feels this way, but I am really encouraged that I am not alone; that I'm not the only one," she says. "My favorites, of course, are the ladies who cover cheerfully and enjoy making coverings and outfits to go with them (or vice-versa). Even if I am having a bad day or week, it's good to know that someone is able to enjoy a good day in their obedience and submission and reverence to God in worship."

A Step Toward Obedience

To women who may be thinking about covering, Lisa says it could be one meaningful step in a life of obedience to God. "Keep an open mind and heart to God's words," she says. "Keep seeking because Jesus said when we seek, we will find. Keep trusting, too, because God does care. Keep doing what you believe to be right. We must be convinced, and we can be, I think. Doing something that seems to be so small is like a catalyst to other things that are good and helpful and that help that light in you to shine. In the Bible, James says 'show me your faith without works, and I will show you my faith by what I do.' If we do one seemingly small thing, then it's easier to do another small thing, and another and another, until we have submitted more and more completely to God's will and design," she says. "Oh, and make sure that you are sharing with your husband – even if he doesn't appear to be

51

listening. Listen to his point of view, since that is a significant part of what this is all about."

Though Lisa doesn't cover full time (she covers mostly during prayer, worship and prophesy), she is no less passionate about covering, and her commitment to it is no less an integral part of her life. She readily admits that head covering is no trivial matter. "Head covering in the Bible is not a subject to be dismissed," she says, "nor is it something on which all the Law and the Prophets hang. It could be assumed that head covering is of little consequence, but I assure you that there are many, many matters of daily living in Christ, which are important to attend to," she says. "Head covering is but one small obedient thing, done by only the women of God's children; one small thing found in a Book full of commands, precepts, laws, prophecies, proverbs, illustrations and wisdom – among other important things. Head covering is one small thing that is often overlooked, misunderstood and even frowned upon in our day. But why should anything, no matter how small, be overlooked, when it comes to living for the One who I believe gave up a heavenly dwelling to live here on earth as a man, and then be treated with contempt and killed in such a horrific way – all for my sake?

"Head covering is one of the many things that comes along at some point in our spiritual growth and appears to those whose hearts are full of seeking. I believe it is shameful to dismiss covering as some 'cultural' thing that we don't need to think about today.

"Oh yes, there's a movement or two afoot," Lisa continues, "and they all seem to be one, really: that swing of the proverbial pendulum, back from extreme liberality in doing whatever we want, toward seeking and finding out what God, the Creator and King, really said and taught

His disciples to write down for us. As we find that feminine behavior is more pleasing to God, we add on modest dress and head covering; or perhaps it is the reverse order. But we continually add on other things as we learn and grow — such as love, patience, self-control and that inner peace and joy that we were designed for, which shine as light to others around us. Maybe we are all on separate paths now, but with prayer and continual seeking, I believe that many of us will find the one Path, because those who seek do find. Those who join a movement because everyone else is doing it won't. But those who are really moving will. So yes, head covering is just one small thing. But so is a cup of water. A child. The rod of Moses. A stone and a sling. A tent peg. An arrow. A visit. A coin. A parchment. Nothing is small. Not really."

*C*hapter 7

A Soul's Profit

Therefore, since we are surrounded by such a great cloud of witnesses, let us throw off everything that hinders and the sin that so easily entangles, and let us run with perseverance the race marked out for us. – Hebrews 12:1

"I remember when I first became an Orthodox Christian," Isidora recalls. "We had in our parish an old woman named Anna. Everyone called her *Babushka* (Grandmother). She was from Russia and had survived World War II mostly in a Russian prison camp as she, pregnant with twins at the time, was caught trying to flee Russia with her son and husband. Her husband was taken to a different camp. She never saw him again.

"At the end of the war, she came with her three children to the United States. She never remarried. As a result of her difficult life, she took her faith very seriously. Babushka always wore a headscarf tied under her little chin. She also dressed modestly in skirts. The only parts of her she didn't cover were her face and hands below the wrists. She was always smiling – a soft, sweet smile," Isidora remembers. "The only time I ever saw her look harshly at someone was when they were immodestly dressed. I was sitting next to her one day after church. A young man was passing by us wearing long pants and sandals with no socks. Babushka took her cane and crunched his toes with it. 'No socks! No good!' she said in her heavy Russian accent. And to this day that man's toes are never naked! She was also known to whack young girls on the legs when their skirts were too short."

It was through the influence of women in the Scriptures, as well as older women in the Orthodox Church that Isidora, 43, came to dress modestly and cover her head at all times. "Babushka was my hero," she says. "I'm neither bold enough, nor interested in, protesting the immodest choices made by other people. For myself, though, I always wear skirts, a head covering and long-sleeved shirts.

"We are instructed by God to enter into holy obedience for the salvation of our souls," she says. "To obey only insofar as we find it agreeable is not profitable for our salvation. We take up our cross and follow. In a world where there is a tendency to think and analyze things to death, there is a feeling of comfort in simply obeying."

An Untraditional Separation

Isidora admits that her decision to cover has played out amidst a rather unusual marital and family situation. Married for 17 years and separated for over 7 years, Isidora and her husband are the parents of two boys. Despite the marital separation, Isidora and her husband still live in the same house. "Within the first year, our marriage went sour due to his infidelity. We are currently living in separate parts of the house," she says. "We stay together because we want to raise the children together in a traditional manner where I stay at home with them. He is inadequate as a husband," she divulges, "but very competent as a father. In 2000, when I first started to cover, he was not thrilled with it, but he respected my choice," she explains. "Several years later he decided he didn't care for it at all. My husband isn't religious; he has never been baptized nor involved in any sort of spirituality. After the marriage went sour, I began to hunger more for God," she says. "I happened to encounter the Orthodox Church and felt instantly at home. I borrowed a scarf for the first service I went to. After the service, I went to the fabric counter at Walmart and bought fabric to make my own covering. The next morning, Sunday, I showed up at church, head covered and asked to be made a Catechumen.

Heartbreak, Spiritual Loss and the Absence of Covering

Isidora's covering journey is unique in that she covered for four years, dropped the practice of it, and then resumed it again recently – after five years. Her early years of covering were often painful ones. "I think the most heartbreaking moment for me was when my husband, who was having an affair at the time, told me I was ridiculous for dressing modestly and wearing a scarf," she recounts. "I crumbled into a thousand pieces. I felt as though I had been abandoned by God, as well as by my husband. I gave up head covering but not dressing modestly. I felt lost for years after that," she says. "Of course God had not abandoned me. I failed the test. I abandoned *Him*. What a terrible spiritual loss. Distancing myself from God through my choice to be disobedient, negligent and spiritually slothful rewarded me with nothing except despair. It's all about making the choice to become something other than a corrupt and unhappy person who is disengaged from the Creator. So I chose – and must choose every minute – to surrender my will, trusting in God to guide me and to make use of me. I made a decision and followed it with action. On went the scarf. I felt connected once again," she says. "There is nothing as horrible or as devastating as distancing oneself from God. Wearing a scarf helps me to reel in my fallen nature. It is an indispensable gift."

Isidora's young sons played an important role in her journey back to covering again. "When I first began covering again after that long lapse, I was a little concerned that my sons would be embarrassed by it," she says. "They weren't. One day after school, they came home to find me in a headscarf, dress and apron. My 9-year-old got a gentle look in his eyes. He walked over to me, wrapped his arms around my waist, and gave me such a hug! I asked him and my 11-year-old if it was okay with them if I went out in public with a scarf, or if it might make them uncomfortable. They told me it was fine by them; that it looked right," she says. "Returning to the practice of veiling has restored and refreshed my soul. Veiling is a physical act that encourages prayer, reminds me that God is ever present, and that I would be a crazy woman if I didn't give myself over to all that is good and profits the soul."

A Prohibited Vocation

Embracing the I Corinthians passage and the ancient tradition of covering as an Eastern Orthodox Christian were Isidora's primary reasons for covering; but it also served as an outward sign of inner devotion and obedience to God, and as a symbol of her hunger for the things of God. But these were met with indifference by her husband's family. "When I first began to cover full time, my husband's family said nothing. They still say nothing. I suspect they feel it would be prying to ask about it. They live in Oklahoma," she says. "I never see them."

Many years ago, when Isidora longed to express her devotion to God in a vocational sense, her father expressed his disdain. "The only family I am connected to is a father who lives in Oklahoma. He is a Christian, but without a church. In my early twenties, I was still unbaptized. I was strongly attracted to Catholicism and wanted to test my vocation as a nun. My dad told me that if I became Catholic, he would disown me. Being my only relative, that was too much for me to bear," she says. "I joined the National Guard and went to college to become a social worker instead. I married my husband, a fellow soldier, three years later. I've not seen my father for seven years. We talk every day, though."

Isidora admits to a distant relationship with her mother. "We moved around a lot when I was growing up," she says. "My parents divorced when I was six. I was eighteen before I saw my mother again. I send cards to her at the appropriate times. That's the extent of our relationship.

Putting Down (Spiritual) Roots

"My father had a series of wives," she continues. "We continued to move on a regular basis," she says. "It's difficult to settle into a groove and feel safe so that you can grow into a well-balanced adult when you don't live in one place for more than a couple of years. It wasn't until I became Orthodox that I finally settled down with myself. Having lived in uncertainty and instability until I was in my late 20s, I came to value stability, tradition and consistency. I had no reservations about accepting all that Orthodox Christianity presented – including head covering. Knowing that God was never changing gave me great comfort," she says. "I find that I am my happiest when I do as He asks without murmuring."

Among the sources from which Isidora draws strength and support, her church is preeminent. "Within the context of Orthodox Christianity, we have many examples of saints and godly women who have set aside convention in favor of following God," she says. Her friends have also proven invaluable. She readily admits that all of her current friends are Orthodox. "My old friends couldn't relate to me as a Christian and went on their way," she says. "I have been blessed to count two very knowledgeable and loving Christian women as friends and cheerleaders. They have helped to keep me focused and from becoming extreme."

The practical effects of head covering have made life a little simpler for many head covering women. Isidora is no exception. "I'm able to get on with my day much more quickly without the burden of styling my hair," she says. "Windy days are no longer a nuisance for me. In winter I don't have to deal with static disrupting my finely textured hair, which can be extremely annoying." It should come as no surprise that the practical effects of covering often evolve into spiritual ones, as well. "With my hair put away, I have nothing to hide under," Isidora says. "I find my interaction with other people to be much more open. I can see them better, both literally and figuratively. My head covering reinforces my conscience, encouraging me to make proper choices. I find myself more inclined to pray. I am more aware of the fact that God and a multitude of witnesses are surrounding me – seen and unseen – and that I would do well to behave accordingly. Wearing a head covering, as I move throughout my day, helps me to check unbecoming behavior and turn instead toward actions befitting a Christian.

"There is a feeling of protection that comes over me when I wear a scarf. I feel immediately strengthened, deep within myself, as I tie the scarf upon my head. The scarf reminds me of my commitment to God; reminds me that I must strive to be a new person and to pray without ceasing.

"From an Orthodox discussion list I found this meaningful quote: "As Fr. Sophrony instructed Fr. Seraphim, 'Read only that which inspires you to prayer.'" And so it is with everything," Isidora says. "Dress in a manner which inspires you to prayer. Speak in a manner which inspires you to prayer. Watch only that which inspires you to prayer."

Chapter 8

A Sign to the Angels and Man

For man did not come from woman, but woman from man... For this reason, and because of the angels, the woman ought to have a sign of authority on her head. – I Corinthians 11:8, 10

"Strangely, the first time I heard of covering was in a Christian chat room," says Kim, a 41-year-old married woman raising four boys. "We had been praying for someone and then someone asked if we had our coverings on. Most of us were a little like, '*Huh*?' The woman cited the I Corinthians 11 passage and the debate began. But the idea of covering never really left me.

"Sometime after this I became curious about the Amish. At that time, they were the only people I knew who covered. But did this mean I had to be Amish to cover? Some years went by, and God began to convict me, in steps, about modesty," she recalls. "I was in long dresses when I began trying to search out this head covering thing.

"I asked my pastor, my friends and my husband's family about it. They all said it wasn't necessary in this day and age. Well, why was I feeling so unsettled in my spirit? When I asked my husband about it, his first reaction was surprise. He told me he had never paid much attention to the I Corinthians passage, as it seemed more a woman's issue. He said that if I felt led by God to do this, then I should go ahead and do it.

"My family didn't care much about covering; they are not Christians, but they were curious.

61

But my husband's Christian family? Oh my!" Kim recalls. "It was a very rough time for both my husband and me. My husband had never seen his mother, who ordinarily has such a quiet demeanor, become so angry. She never shared why she was so angry, but the change in her was startling. She seems to have now accepted where we are, even if she doesn't agree with our lifestyle.

"So, in the beginning, I had to take all of these responses into account. I kept going back and forth on the whole covering thing. I heard what everyone was telling me, but my head and heart were telling me something different. One day, in desperation, I asked God if He would allow me to meet a covered woman face to face to ask her questions. Up to that point, all I had read online was from a man's point of view. I wanted to know what was it really like to cover, from a woman's perspective, and did a woman really *have* to do it? This felt like a really tall order at the time, because the only women I knew to cover were the Amish, Mennonites, Catholic nuns and Muslim women.

"But, oh, the Lord blessed me so!" Kim continues, excitedly. "I was with my children in Michael's craft store. I thought I saw a lady with something white on her head. I was so excited; I tried getting the boys to rush, so we wouldn't lose her. I didn't have to hunt for long before I caught up with her. Her name was Lori, and my first question was whether or not she was a Mennonite. She said she wasn't. Then I asked her if she would mind some questions from a complete stranger about her covering. She told me she wouldn't mind.

"It is amazing to me now how God worked things out! She was there dropping off her older two children for their art class, so we had time to talk. We stood there in the aisle talking for about an hour. She told me she covered merely because of the directive from Scripture to do so; the church she attended did not practice covering. In fact, her pastor had been trying to take subtle jabs at her from the pulpit, in order to release her from her 'legalism'. Her husband was not a Christian, but he wasn't opposed to her covering. She told me of the positive changes that covering had brought about in her life. It was this woman's witness, and the fact that she didn't belong to a church where head covering was practiced that really spurred me on to cover. And since my husband was fine with it, I started with a white bandana that I bought at Michael's craft store. I wore a veil for some time, but was often mistaken for a nun. This veil was also similar to the head coverings worn by a group I considered almost cult-like. I didn't want to be confused as either. This is why I began wearing the kapp style (a bonnet-like covering which has a brimmed crown, beneath which the mass of hair is placed).

Challenging Realizations

Kim has now covered for over four years, and covers all the time. Her covering has positively influenced both her marriage and her life, but it has also brought to light truths about her that are difficult to face. "My husband has become stronger in his conviction that a woman should cover," she says, "and we are able to discuss spiritual things more freely with each other now. But I have to say, personally, it has been harder, because I realize how I haven't been very submissive, and it has been a battle," she concedes. "I want to submit, but my flesh fights it so much. I wonder if this is something I am always going to struggle with. Some days I feel as if I am treating my husband like one of the children. I want victory. I do not say this lightly. I want to be victorious. In many ways my husband is a gentle man; he rarely gets angry – the polar opposite of me. There are times when I am very conscious of it, and have it on my mind to think before I act, but so very often I let my guard down. I can really relate to Paul's inner battle spoken of in Romans, chapter 7."

Though covering has made a lasting impact on her life, Kim is still challenged by the difficulty of not imposing her standards onto others. "I never want to judge another person for not covering," she says. "I have to be reminded of that again and again. I have to look at myself and remember how much I sin. I am very aware of my own shortcomings."

The Fruit of Obedience

One of Kim's greatest joys is knowing that she finally responded in obedience in the call to cover. "That nagging in my spirit was gone. I felt such peace. My husband was able to sense this, and said he had never known me to be so full of peace. Also, I was able to read Scripture like I never had before. It was like my eyes were opened to it for the first time," she says. "It all seemed so alive to me. How can I disregard I Corinthians 11:1-16, but follow the precepts regarding communion in that very same chapter?"

Though in the early days of her covering Kim and her family did not attend a church where head covering was practiced, they are now members of the Old Order River Brethren, and the support reinforces Lisa's commitment to covering. "At our church we are reminded *why* we cover," she says. "I have been sad to find that there are some who cover who just do it, no longer remembering *why* – other than they know

that it is a sign of nonconformity to the world.
Now that we are a part of a church that practices
full time covering, covering is just a part of
getting dressed," she says. "But I do not ever
want to get to the point of complacency about it.
Just as we are to put on the spiritual armor, I put
on my covering – as a sign to the angels and
man."

Chapter 9

Obedience and Cultural Comfort

Wives, submit to your husbands as to the Lord. For the husband is the head of the wife as Christ is the head of the church, his body, of which he is the Savior. Now as the church submits to Christ, so also wives should submit to their husbands in everything. – Ephesians 5:22-24

"My husband and I were having a casual discussion with another Christian couple, whom we didn't know very well, after visiting my in-laws' church. The husband of the other couple said, 'And, really, why *do* we ignore certain passages? You know, like women covering their heads to pray?!' My husband – who has two seminary degrees – and I looked at each other and said, 'Yeah – why *do* we ignore that one?' So we began by separately reading I Corinthians 11. He thought it seemed more like a command we have no reason to disobey, and I came back to him with the same opinion after reading it myself. Then I did a lot of research in his theological library and online. I later studied the early church fathers, leaders of the Protestant Reformation, and scholars of today, as well as current pastors' studies, sermons, writings, and the online writings of other women who cover their heads to pray. I found no good reason to disobey. So I obey."

Sandra is 29 years old, and has been married to her husband for over five years. They are both missionaries in Costa Rica. Sandra grew up in Michigan in a non Conservative Mennonite church, which she says is better described as Anabaptist with pacifist beliefs, and no particular regulations regarding coverings or dress. In college she began attending a church which belongs to the General Association of Regular Baptist Churches (GARBC).

Sandra has covered for only a few months, and covers her head for any prayer she is involved in during which it is obvious that she is praying, such as in church or with her husband at home – whether or not she is the one speaking the prayer. "I also cover my head when I read Scripture aloud," She says. "And lastly, I always cover when I am singing songs directed to God – hymns, psalms and spiritual songs – because they are often prayers in my heart to Him."

As with many women who cover, Sandra does not limit her covering to her head alone. "I have nearly always dressed in ways I consider modest," she says. "Although it isn't that I'm always wearing long skirts and turtle necks. I do often wear long skirts – a practice I started probably two years ago when I realized that wearing them reminds me of my position in our home. I am not the same as my husband. He is in charge and I am his help-meet. Also, when I started wearing skirts for myself, my husband started telling me how much he liked them and adored how feminine I looked. Now I wear a skirt almost every day, and he still loves it."

A Husband's Support

Sandra's husband has not only lent her invaluable support since the inception of her covering journey, but he remains an integral part of her journey's day-to-day practicalities. "He definitely stands by our decision that I cover," she says. "Often, he'll bring me my head covering when it's time to pray, which is very sweet. We still need to truly study exactly *when* covering is necessary, since he isn't convinced that I must cover my head for prayer at home," she admits. "But he is wonderfully supportive and believes that if my understanding is that I should cover my head for prayer times when we are at home, I had better do it, so that I'm not sinning in my heart."

Sandra says that responses and perceptions from in-laws, friends and blood relatives comprise an interesting mix of feedback regarding her covering. "My mother apparently wore a head covering when she and my father were first married, because at that time the Mennonite Church was requiring it of members. She doesn't really remember why she stopped or exactly when, but didn't think much about it for herself. She is generally supportive of me, though I perceive that she might think I'm a little 'out there'. When we went to a women's luncheon put on by her church, she was quite supportive and helped to make sure I had something to cover my head during prayer. My father passed away before I started covering. My father's sister found it 'interesting' that I'm doing it and she sent me an email saying that she did it for a while, when it was required at church, but really didn't think it is for today and is quite comfortable not wearing one. But if I want to, she said, that's nice.

"My father-in-law hasn't said much, but my mother-in-law seems to think it's an interesting idea – for *me* to do it – but that it's not really a command in Scripture, and it's pretty clear that she's not as 'strange' as I am, so won't be joining anytime soon.

"My husband's sister has very strict beliefs on many issues within Christianity, including proper roles for husbands and wives and she does submit to her husband. However, we haven't discussed head covering much, since I think she doesn't want to study it for fear of conviction," Sandra says, light-heartedly.

"My brothers aren't following God very closely right now, though each attended a semester of college at Christian institutions. One hasn't said anything, and the other discussed it with me briefly, trying to convince me that it's not for today.

"My new friends, whom I met just a few days after starting to cover my head, were very supportive, overall. They understood my conviction, even though none of them felt compelled to join me in the journey. I started my blog as a way to talk about what I was learning and to communicate with others. I was quite encouraged by a lady who rather strongly disagreed, but said that she respected me for holding to my convictions, even though she could see that it wasn't easy. My friends back in my home city followed the blog to some extent, but we really haven't had opportunities for interaction about it, since I returned home for only a couple of months, packed all of our things, and moved overseas. Here in Costa Rica, I'm sort of short on friends," Sandra confesses, "and we don't usually discuss anything substantive; and that's kind of sad. But I do still connect with my friends via email."

Though Sandra admits that she is not 'technically' a part of a head covering church or denomination, her pastor was recently forthcoming about his advocacy of covering. "Just a few weeks after I started covering my head, while I was still half way across the country, the pastor of my home church was teaching on men's and women's roles within the structure of the church and church authority. As he taught, he used I Corinthians 11, and since his format allowed for questions, someone asked for his opinion on head coverings. He said that he could find no biblical reason for women *not* to cover their heads for prayer, and that it seemed to him to be a command to cover their heads. Since then, a few women – including one who grew up covering and had stopped for a time, as well as the pastor's unmarried daughters – have begun to cover their heads during church services," she says. "What incredible timing for my return to the church as someone wearing a head covering and dreading the stares and questions. God provided comfort for me in an amazing way!"

Appropriate Times to Cover

Since Sandra doesn't cover full-time, she faces unique challenges not common for women who cover most or all of the time. "One of my greatest challenges is figuring out exactly which situations call for me to cover my head," she says. She says that she plans to give more in-depth study time to finding out what proper situations require head covering, and to then ensure she always has something handy with which to cover. "In a pinch, I have used napkins or an extra item of clothing nearby," she says. "Often, I have chosen to wear sweaters with hoods, which I put up for prayer and, of course, I often use the scarves that I have nearby for this purpose. Also, my favorite solution for when someone 'prays on me'", she offers, humorously, "is my husband's hand on my head. I'm getting better at guessing when someone might pray, and having a head covering easily accessible. But there are times when I'm just not ready – like when I'm helping someone prepare a meal in her kitchen, and suddenly the rest of the group enters the room and then the host prays, thanking God for our food and fellowship. Usually my husband is already standing near me. So I 'duck' my head into him or nudge him and he puts his hand on my head. I don't believe this is the best option for most prayer times, but I decided that it is a good representation of the symbolism in God's command to cover my head to pray, and that if my husband is the one who is literally covering my head, it is no doubt a sign of my submission to him and functions well when it is the least disruptive option in such a situation."

Sowing Seeds

One of Sandra's most memorable joys in her head covering journey is seeing the way God prepared the soil for the head covering seeds He would later sow in her heart. "During our trip to the Middle East last summer, I happened to buy a very plain, but beautiful scarf which the ladies there often use to cover their heads, whether they are Orthodox Jews or Muslims. I bought it in the Old City of Jerusalem, which gives it special meaning to me. It is also lightweight, easy to fold, doesn't wrinkle and looks attractive with my skin tone," she says. "Remember, I was not covering my head when I bought it, and I really didn't know what I'd do with it once I returned to the States. I just liked it. My husband also encouraged me to buy a few pretty *Pashmina* scarves in Jordan, simply because he liked the way they looked; he didn't know what we'd do with those, either! Now they are special occasion scarves. To be clear, I don't wear scarves on my head to attract attention; in fact, I hope for quite the opposite. But I do try to wear scarves that don't clash with my clothing, since that would attract *more* attention."

To the woman who is new to covering, Sandra offers insightful advice: "Don't let people's questions dissuade you. They are probably just curious or attempting to avoid covering their own heads and thus seem 'against' you. Work on memorizing the text of I Corinthians 11:1-16. It will help you remain steadfast in your new convictions and give you the best answer you could ever have to address the questions which are bound to come your way. And, most of all, don't forget that covering is an outward sign of how God wants your heart to be: submissive to your husband. Make sure that you don't ruin the symbol of the church's submission to Christ or Christ's submission to the Father. Submit cheerfully to your husband in *everything*. And yes, it's easier said than done. Just ask my husband. Occasionally, I rebel," she admits. "But that's sinning, so I have to ask for both my husband's and God's forgiveness and pledge to improve in the next moments with God's help."

To women who are thinking about covering, she offers counsel no less enlightened: "Just do it. It's not comfortable. But the Bible doesn't promise cultural comfort; God commands obedience to His Word and He promises His faithfulness, peace and love.

Chapter 10

Signs of Godly Femininity

*Love the Lord your God with all your heart and
with all your soul and with all your strength.
These commandments that I give you today are
to be upon your hearts. Impress them on your
children. Talk about them when you sit at home
and when you walk along the road, when you lie
down and when you get up. Tie them as symbols
on your hands and bind them on your foreheads.
Write them on the doorframes of your houses
and on your gates.* –Deuteronomy 6:5-9

Something was missing. But Sanil, 23, had yet
to find out what that something was. "I had
mostly left the church when I discovered
Messianic Judaism," she says. "I believed in God,
and considered myself a Christian, but felt
uncomfortable and attacked in actual churches,
so I had no real community, and I was drifting.
During my senior year of college, I started slowly
getting back into church by going to small group
studies," she says. "These helped me a lot. One of
these was a Jewish roots study, taught by a
Messianic Jew. I had never heard that term used
before, but I was very interested in the things he
taught and I wanted to learn more." Sanil says
she researched Messianic resources and groups
and began to learn more about Messianic
Judaism. The missing piece finally fell into place;
Sanil knew this was something she could commit
to – something that would forever change the
landscape of her religious life.

Not Your Average Church Girl

Messianic Judaism was quite different from anything Sanil had been taught while growing up in church. For Sanil, this had much to do with the distinctions made between the First and Second (or Old and New) Testaments in her church experience. "The Torah (the most sacred and revered teachings of the Bible's First Testament) would be used," she says of the teaching in her previous churches, "but it was thought that most of it didn't apply. It was all a cultural code meant for Jews, and we were free to break it, because we weren't under the Law anymore. The emphasis was on the New Testament – this is what really mattered." Sanil says that following definitive practices and traditions was something that was lacking in her previous church experience. "Messianic Judaism was different; I learned that the Torah has a beauty and value that are still significant for my life today. I believe that *all* of Scripture is inspired of God and can be learned from. The New (or Second) Testament is very important for me in shaping my beliefs and behavior. In Judaism, I have Scriptures and rich, observable customs. I have rituals that remind me of and connect me with the Jews throughout history, rituals that Yeshua (the Hebrew or Aramaic name for Jesus) probably practiced, as well. I am not solitary anymore."

Pleasing God

Sanil, a single graduate student studying Theology, with a concentration in Biblical Studies, began covering after she had stumbled upon head covering websites and started to consider whether or not she should embrace the practice herself. It followed that dressing modestly just made sense. "If I'm concerned with pleasing God and being humble and modest, why would I continue to dress in a worldly way that draws attention to my appearance? Also, apart from how others see me, the way I dress also affects my attitude," she observes. "When I wear low-cut shirts and put too much time into my clothes and hair, I know my heart is not in the right place, that I care about how others see me, and have a desire to be seen as beautiful physically, rather than to be seen as humbly following God. When I'm dressed this (worldly) way, it's easier to give into unholy thoughts and actions. On the other hand, when I make an effort to dress in a way that is pleasing to God, it is a constant reminder to continue that desire in my thoughts and actions. When I wear a head covering, it's a visible and tactile sign for myself – that I have made the commitment to change my actions and to serve God with them," she says. "I do also believe that the Bible (both the Torah and New Testament) suggests that women should cover their heads, although these passages are somewhat ambiguous and I understand that many do not read them that way. I see covering and dressing modestly as signs and actions of godly femininity, showing humility and submission and a desire to live according to God's will, and to fill the role He has for us. I realize that this step is not for everyone, but it is right for me. I believe that God is leading me in this direction, and I intend to follow Him in it."

Life Outside the Box

Sanil, who describes herself as painfully shy, readily admits that the perceptions of others was among her chief challenges when she first began covering. "Initially I had trouble being brave enough to go outside wearing the head covering and, to a smaller extent, the more modest style of dressing I've adopted. Some friends encouraged me to overcome my fears the first few times, and once I was out and people were looking, it quickly stopped being strange. I think I realized that people were looking at me oddly and that they would in the future, but that was the extent of it," she says. "Also, I found a weird confidence in it. I've always been afraid of speaking my mind, for fear that other people would think what I have to say is useless or stupid. When I knew people were looking at me, and that I was willing to stick with covering anyway, I was less shy about speaking. They already think I'm odd; why not let them hear what I have to say, instead of letting them draw conclusions based only on appearance?"

For many women who cover, dealing with the anxiety brought on by the perceptions of strangers pales in comparison with the apprehension felt when relatives are told about the decision to cover. "When I was home on a break from school, some of the scarves I had ordered were mistakenly shipped to my home address, rather than my school address. So, I told my mom about it and tried wearing one of the scarves to church one morning, and she was visibly upset by it and asked me why I was wearing it. Not wanting to start an in-depth religious discussion at the moment – it's a sore enough subject at home, as it is – I told her I liked them. She told me that I couldn't wear it to church, and I understood by how upset she was that I shouldn't wear them at all while I was at home," she says. "While I was home, I covered my hair with smaller bandanas or put it up in a ponytail – not something I was entirely comfortable with, as I felt very exposed after my time covering. But since I feel that covering is not actually a mandatory Biblical command, I felt that keeping the peace at home and honoring my mother's feelings about it were more important.

During that break, we did discuss my religious beliefs," she continues. "She still doesn't understand them, but she's trying. I expect this will be a slow process, but if I can keep the process going, I hope to be able to further explain my beliefs and practices so that I can behave with her the same as I do on my own, without either of us being afraid or angry about it."

What Sanil seems to lack in family support is well made up in her network of close friends. "My friends are extremely supportive," she says. "At one time or another, most of them have asked me why I cover. Occasionally, they seem to forget that I cover even while they are talking to me, asking if I want to go shopping for bathing suits or go to the pool. I politely remind them I'm not going to do those things, but will go with them and sit nearby, and then they usually understand and let it drop."

Though Sanil's covering journey has thus far been brief, it has noticeably matured her. "I have developed a lot spiritually, and have come to realize some of the things I was doing wrong. Covering has made me more humble and open, and it's given me an understanding of God that I didn't have before," she says. "I speak more in class, and to other people. I think I smile more and am generally friendlier. I make much more of an effort to spend a lot of time in prayer and worship than I had in the past."

Sanil embraces covering with an unmistakable passion and whole-hearted conviction, and she has no plans of ever losing that. "I plan to cover for the rest of my life," she says. "There are times when I start to doubt this, and the covering seems silly. I get tired of standing out in a crowd, of having everyone know my name (and knowing it's because I look different from everyone else in this city) when I can't remember ever being introduced to them. And I get tired of not being able to talk to my family about it, because I feel like that should be a major source of support, and for me, it often winds up being more of a hindrance. At these times, I want to tear off the head coverings, pack them away in a box, and just try to be like my mom wants me to be," she concedes. "But this is not honest; I don't really feel it would be right. While I feel it would be acceptable, and that covering is not something I *have* to do, I do feel like it is something I am *lead* to do. When I see friends of mine with beautiful hair styles and clothes that I couldn't wear, sometimes I get a little jealous, but this also helps cement in my mind that I am doing the right thing for me. I want to stop trying to look good for other people, and instead concern myself about what my heart looks like to God. By covering myself up and not playing the fashion game, I know that I won't be tempted to be drawn into silly, superficial concerns, and can be devoted to more important things. It's unfortunate that this decision makes me stand out, but following God is countercultural many times. I am trying very hard to get used to that and to not let it bother me.

"One of the ways covering has changed me is that I know I am visible – whether I want to be or not. People have different expectations when they see a woman in a head covering. It continually makes me aware of how short I fall of those standards. While I don't want to become legalistic and be caught up in my shortcomings, I do feel it's important that I have been made aware that I need to change in a way I wasn't aware of before. It's one thing to say you want to follow God, and to take a few steps to change something like your clothing," she says. "But if the heart isn't really there, and you haven't developed the behavior and attitude to match, then the head covering is silly, because it doesn't mean anything. Modesty is much more than dress," she offers. "I'm trying to make modesty more of a spiritual concern, adjusting my heart so that my inside matches my clothing choices, and my outside is a reflection of my heart."

*C*hapter 11

Men Folk on the Journey

The secret things belong to the Lord our God, but the things revealed belong to us and to our children forever, that we may follow all the words of this law. – Deuteronomy 29:29

When I was a sophomore in college, my mother moved to a quaint little section of my hometown. I loved all the tall brick houses and the lush fullness of the trees in her new neighborhood. When I was home during semester breaks, I enjoyed taking long walks in that aged and scenic neighborhood, and as I would walk, I would talk with God. There was a seminary there in my mother's new neighborhood, and I longed to be inside its walls. I was a new Christian then and burning with holy fire for Christ. Back on campus I was involved with Bible studies, Christian fellowship groups and the active practice of learning to share my faith. I was sold out.

As I would walk past this seminary, I passed it with a thirst difficult to describe. I wanted in. I wanted at it. I longed to learn whatever godly thing that might be taught there. I was meant for Christ, meant for His work – I think I knew that even then. I wasn't sure exactly what that work might look like, but I was taking applications. Attending seminary seemed like a reasonable enough start for me. Oh, how I dreamed of toiling for Christ, steeped in my Christian vocation!

During one of those walks back then, a thought came over me. Suppose I were to attend seminary? Suppose I were to fill up on the knowledge found in the dusty old books I would read there? Suppose I were to walk out the depth of my calling and grow rich in wisdom? What would that mean for the man whom I might marry? What if I ended up knowing more than he would, being more spiritual than he? What if my spiritual hunger were more voracious than his? Silly thought, I know; but that didn't stop me from thinking it.

Even now, twenty years later, I can still remember how defining those questions were for me back then. I wanted to marry and have a family; that much I knew. It didn't seem fitting that I would be a spiritual brick house while the man in my life were some forlorn, religious old shack. Of course, that didn't have to be the case (I might have married someone I thought my spiritual equal or even superior), but I was terribly concerned that it might be. So, I backed down. I held back. I tried not to know, so that – *somehow* – he would know more. I became less so that he – *whomever he might be*! – could become more. In this way, I reasoned, I could prepare for the future and be the sort of 'following' wife a 'leader' husband should have.

The Authentic You

I tried 'not to know' then, and I spent a number of years thereafter trying 'not to know'. The problem, though, is that small droplets of who you truly are will seep through the fabric of the person God has called you to be. The more you try to dab it dry, the more the godly spill bleeds through. You keep trying to blot it, but you're only left with a stream that widens and darkens. One day you awaken and there is no denying the beautiful, bubbling brook that is welling up inside of you, yearning for further release. One day you wake up and you become *true*.

And it's okay to be true. It's good to be true. You can still honor your husband, your brother, your son or your father if you are true. You needn't deny who you are. You simply must be gentle with it. Contrary to popular belief, a man is a sensitive thing. His pride is sometimes easily wounded. He searches for solutions. He uses logic. His logical arguments are often threatening. He wants to be right. He wants to take the lead. He wants you to follow. He wants to be your hero.

If you find one day that you feel lead to cover, and you talk about it with your husband (brother, son, father, and so on) and he advocates and affirms your decision to cover right from the start, get on your knees right now and thank God, because it's likely you are in the minority. Most of us have had to juggle our own inner doubts and his, as well. It's not easy.

A Place for Mystery

Last Sunday in church my dear pastor spoke about the value of mystery. Indeed, there is a place for mystery throughout the course of our spiritual lives, but we have to be willing to embrace it. When it comes to mystery, we have to be generous, open-handed. We can't be tight-fisted with mystery. That's not how it works. But if we are willing, if we are seeking, we may discover in this mystery something far more important than having all the answers. We serve a God who is both disclosed and mysterious. Should we serve only the aspect of God which we think we understand perfectly and not worship the part of Him which is yet mysterious? In I Corinthians 13, the apostle Paul says we know in part and we prophesy in part, but when perfection comes, the imperfect disappears (verses 9 and 10). There are just some things we won't understand as long as we dwell in these mortal frames.

Perhaps the men in our lives had hoped to have all the answers – or at least a good number of them. Maybe mystery interrupted their lives in much the same way it intercepted ours. It's what we do with this mystery, how we respond to this mystery, that marks our lives. Will we go kicking and screaming? Will we be angry? Will we grow bitter in the fog of mystery, feeling we *deserve* to understand?

We Just Have to Obey

I have to admit, I love the way men and women are designed; theirs is a colorful combination. There are some things that my husband does that I wouldn't want to touch with a ten foot pole. And there are some things that I take care of which are better left in my capable hands. My husband is good with his hands, and I often tell many of our friends there is nothing he can't fix. But he couldn't fix my desire to cover. I think he wanted to, though. I think he wanted to understand, wanted to make me see how this very little thing really isn't that big of a deal; that, ultimately, it's just not that important. But in my spirit, I sensed God was saying otherwise. Did I understand it? By all means, no – not at all! But we don't have to understand, do we? We just have to obey.

This is not that part of the book where I tell you to disregard your husband's view should he tell you not to cover, when you believe God called you to it. I don't think that's my place. I know that if my husband had ever been vehemently opposed to it, I probably wouldn't have covered. Most times he likes to see my hair, while other times he's entirely fine with my covering. Admittedly, it's a delicate balance which requires thoughtful judgment on my part. I think he is beginning to understand that this new conviction of mine doesn't make him any less my hero. It's not always that our men want to deny us of something so important to us. I think that sometimes they are afraid to lose parts of us to something else. I really don't know how to say it more plainly than that. Perhaps he has hurt you with some of the things he has said about covering. Maybe he told you that you weren't hearing from God, or that the whole idea of covering in this day and age is ridiculous. Perhaps you can't understand why your husband – a faithful follower of Christ – can't (or won't) think more spiritually about so meaningful a thing. He may have even told you outright that he will not tolerate you covering your head. In some cases, I honestly think what he is really saying to you is *"Why can't I just be enough for you?"*

Discerning His Need and Learning His Language

Remember the story of Hannah in I Samuel chapter 1? Hannah had no children, while her husband's other wife, Peninnah, had children. Penny used to provoke Hannah, and all Hannah really wanted was a child. Did you catch what Hannah's husband, Elkanah, said to her in verse 8? I honestly don't think Elkanah wanted to deny Hannah of children. He just wanted to be enough for her. "Don't I mean more to you than ten sons?" he asks her in the latter part of verse 8.

And I'm not just speculating here. My dear husband has told me on more than one occasion that he wanted to be my 'everything'. No, it's not logical, nor is it probably even healthy! But that doesn't stop our men from *feeling* it. You might wonder why they won't just come out and *say* what they feel – it would save us a world of

misery, wouldn't it? But that's where our
sensitivity must come into play. This is when we
need to rely upon the Holy Spirit to give us
wisdom and discernment: during those very
critical moments our men aren't saying what they
really feel. One of the things I've found beneficial
in my covering journey is learning to speak my
husband's language. Actually, it's not just *his*
language; it's the language we have developed
together during the course of our 15 year
marriage. It's the way we say things, the context
in which say them and our motive for saying
them. Sometimes it's a look or a gesture, a tone
or an attitude. All of these can comprise our
'language' with someone, and that language can
be good and edifying, or it can be negative and
self-seeking.

My wonderful husband and I have a humorous
language. It's often comical because my husband
enjoys humor and laughter so much. I'm much
more serious and contemplative, and humor
helps to balance me out. Our language has been
built, to some degree, on the funny twist we give
to some of the everyday things we encounter – a
movie we've seen, a conversation we've
overheard, or even a concept we want to expand
and adopt into our general language. For
instance, we think that the English language is
lacking when it comes to terms used to define
deep and abiding love. You can say, "I love God"
and "I love Italian food", and the same word
(love) is used for both statements. Of course, one
could guess that a person's love for God is greater
(or at least it should be!) than a person's love for
Italian food. So, together, we created the word
iuka (*eye-YOO-kah*). To you, dear ones, it holds
no real meaning; but to my husband and me, it
means the highest form of love, commitment and
total devotion a married couple can experience.

So in holiday cards we exchange we often use the word "iuka" to express our feelings of love. Similarly, someone told my husband some years back (if I'm remembering this correctly!) that if you mouth the words 'olive juice' it looks the same as if you were to mouth the words 'I love you'. (You just tried it, didn't you? Already, I know you so well, beloved!). So sometimes when my husband and I send text messages back and forth to each other, we will use the words 'olive juice' as a fun spin on the phrase 'I love you'. And when have disappointed the other in some way, we might go to the other and say, "I should have known better. I can't do *nothin'* right!!" which might really mean, "I'm sorry. Please forgive me and encourage me, and tell me it's no big deal."

Beloved, find that language between you and him – be it verbal, physical or a little bit of both – and use that language to affirm him. Only you can say what needs to be said in a way that he will appreciate and understand. Only you can perform that special service that will help him to remember he is as important to you as ever. Only you can bask in his presence in a way that is fulfilling to him and will enable him to know he doesn't take a back seat to head covering.

Our gentleness, our love and our sensitivity can often win our men over. This doesn't mean that we are trying to manipulate them. Let's be clear: we are not putting on an 'act' so that we can get what we want. It's about so much more than that, dear ones. In Philippians chapter 2, verses 3-4, we are exhorted to *do nothing out of selfish ambition or vain conceit, but in humility consider others better than yourselves. Each of you should look not only to your own interests, but also to the interest of others.* Head covering is about much more than putting some cloth on our heads and walking around acting spiritually superior to others. Thankfully, most of the head covering women I know are far from this unhealthy model. If new birth in Christ has changed our lives at all for the better – having transformed us into more loving, humble, yielded and selfless servants of Christ, head covering should do this all the more. It should remind us of the beauty of God's natural order. It should remind us that we are not the ones in control. It should help us remember that it's a good thing to honor our husbands and to grow in submission to them, even when the world calls us weak because of it. It's not that we agree with everything our husbands say. It's not that we think all of his decisions are the right ones. But one thing we do know: we are ultimately entrusting our lives to God when we walk in obedience to His Word – including His command to honor and lovingly submit to our husbands. An old college friend of mine once told me that if you have to struggle, it's better to struggle *within* the will of God rather than *outside* of it. There may be hard days of following your husband's lead. But in the end, it will go better with you than *not* following it. In the end, whether you cover or end up not covering at all, you can't lose if you are entrusting your destiny to God.

*C*hapter 12

The Wide-Eyed Ride

You shall know the truth, and the truth shall make you odd. – Flannery O'Conner

When I was first sensing the call to cover, I chose a couple of friends with whom to share my heart. I don't blame my friends for finding unusual this new direction I wanted to take. One friend kindly chided me, telling me that I wasn't like those "other" women who wore clothes that were too tight or too revealing. She meant well, but she was implying that I really didn't need to change anything. But I gently explained to her that I was aware, now as never before, of the true condition of my heart. I now understood the true motives behind wearing the clothes that I wore. I told her I was now aware of my vanity and wanted to live in more pure devotion to the Lord. I thought I was allowing my faith to affect every area of my life, but I was wrong. I didn't realize just how much I was holding back.

You Are Not Alone

It's crazy enough that you wake up one day and feel lead of God to cover your head. And it may feel absolutely preposterous when you decide that you intend to be obedient (even though you might not totally understand it). But it's quite another thing entirely to work up the nerve to tell your husband; to toss out subtle hints to co-workers; to tell your women's Bible study group; to explain it to your kids or to walk out in public with your head covered. It's no easy road.

But take courage. You are not the first woman who has dealt with the all delicacies and complexities of entering the world of head covering and, chances are, you won't be the last. Be encouraged that you don't have to do the journey alone, though it may feel like it at first. Once you have connected with other women like yourself, you will feel much better. That's the whole purpose of this book. If God has called you to this He will certainly give you the strength to walk it out, and He will, most assuredly, be right there beside you.

It's a big, scary world out there, and at some point you have to venture out into it as a covered woman of God. This is, in itself, a challenge, because everywhere we turn we see that covering is not the standard of the American culture we live in. In so many other ways, we fit right in with the current culture – we have cell phones, laptops, too many shoes, eat too much, are competitive, ambitious and Facebook members.

Unfortunately, we are moreover challenged, because covering is often not the standard of American *Christian* culture either. In so many ways, we fit right in with the current Christian culture – we have cell phones, laptops, too many shoes, eat too much, are competitive, ambitious and church members. Since we fit right along in so many ways, this one little thing will make us stand out. We may well ask ourselves, "Am I sure I really want to do this?" It can be downright intimidating, especially when we factor in the fact that covering isn't understood, advocated or even talked about in most Christian circles.

Some of us live in diverse communities where we often see Indian, Muslim and Christian women who cover. In such communities, we don't particularly stand out as head covering women. I live in such a community. I often wear head wraps in ways that are commonly seen among African-American women. Most days this is a grace. But there are other days that I want people to ask why my head is covered in such a way. It's strange: some of us blend in so well that we long to be different, and others of us are so different, and we long to blend in.

I will say, though, that I suspect some of my friends from my church have doubtless thought "I can't remember the last time I saw that girl's hair! What on earth is she *doing*??" I think church is probably the one place where I do stand out. Or maybe it just feels that way. My church is predominantly African-American, and it's common to see women in dresses or pant suits with a matching hat (bag, shoes... you get the idea); this is particularly true of the older ladies. I am not in this group, however; my covering always complements my clothing, but it is a cloth covering, not a hat, so in this way there is a distinction. There are not many women in my church who wear head wraps. I've been trying to start a trend there, but so far my efforts haven't proved successful!

The Spirit of Covering

Wherever you are – church, the grocery store, the gym, work or your child's school – you are bound to get looks, stares and even questions at some point. Don't be too uptight about these, and always be courteous and kind. It will go a long way in confirming the virtue of the cloth in the lives of its wearers. People are curious, and most times they mean no harm. Make it your business to put on Christ (Romans 13:14) and to walk in faithfulness to Him.

Occasionally, you may have to deal with negative comments from others – even Christians sometimes. There is beauty and freedom in the fact that we never need to argue them down. We don't need to prove that we are right and they are wrong – God gets no glory in this. The spirit of covering is gentle; it's reverent, kind, submissive, humble and obedient. These are what you put on when you cover. There is no room for pride. Stay as far as you can from self-exaltation and the condemnation of others. People are allowed their own opinions, and you can be sure they will always have them. But don't let people's opinions about you undo you. Their opinions don't define you. Those opinions don't give you your identity or add to your value. You don't answer to the opinions of others. You answer to God. The covering journey is not always a feel good stroll. There may be days of inner struggle and doubt. There may be days when you don't understand why on earth you are doing this. There may be days when you fumble and trip over words in your attempts to explain why covering is so important to you. And many will tell you covering is not necessary. And there may be days you tell yourself the same. Some days you are stronger and other days you are weaker. But Christ is beside you and in you and lives through you. He cares about this pilgrimage of yours; rest in this knowledge, beloved.

Steps in the Journey

This beautiful journey is a series of steps: sensing the call to cover; deciding that you will respond to that call; dealing with your own doubt; talking it over with your husband; sharing your decision with close friends, family and members of your church; your first time out in public with your covering on; your persistent (and sometimes maddening!) attempts to find the style of covering that suits you best; remaining at a church where covering isn't practiced or endorsed, and doing so without the least bit of resentment and, finally, enjoying deeper intimacy with Christ and receiving the satisfying rewards of walking in obedience.

This journey can also be a plethora of possibilities: curiosity about covering; desiring to cover; deciding covering may not be the path you choose to follow; sensing the call to cover, and wanting to cover while dealing with your spouse's objection to it; deciding when the appropriate times are to cover; inspiring other women to cover; forming a support network for other women who decide to cover, or are considering covering. I'm not saying that all the steps and possibilities are easy ones. For this reason, and so many others, you should be very prayerful (and never stop praying!) about the decision to cover.

The Courage to Be

Whether you decide to cover all the time or only at certain times, you will likely deal with varying responses from those you know. Some of those responses may be welcomed and encouraging, while others are decidedly not. We must be patient with our spouses, friends and family who seem baffled by our decision to cover. Despite the fact that many women who cover are anything but obnoxious and dogmatic, some spouses, friends and family members still seem oddly offended. We ourselves think it such a small thing: just a piece of cloth on our heads. We're not trying to strangle anyone with it. We're not trying to handcuff anyone with it. We just want to wear it on our heads as a symbol of our submission, our reverence, our devotion to God, and our recognition of authority.

Okay, confession time: I haven't told many of my family members that I cover. Many do notice that my head is often covered, but probably assume I'm making a personal fashion statement. All of my closest friends know I cover, and they know the reasons why. But I'd be lying if I said I wasn't a wimp when it comes to informing people of this life change. If you are anything like me (and pray you are not!), when it comes to telling someone that you cover, you dance around the subject until you can't avoid it any longer. It must be pulled and pried from you. Then you confess, only to watch the person sit there and stare at you with a quizzical look on his or her face. You don't go banging on family members' doors, about to burst from head covering excitement, enthusiastically ready to share with them the head covering 'gospel'. Nor are you trying to convert all your girlfriends. Still, when you talk about it, you get "the look."

When all is said and done, it might be easier to be a Christian lottery winner than to be a head covering Christian in a postmodern age. Your pastor might not like the way you got the lottery money, but he likely won't turn away your tithes and offerings. Even Christian family members and friends might find it easier to congratulate you on something of worldly significance, like a lucrative job promotion or a move to an expansive house in a posh neighborhood, than on something of spiritual significance.

Love and Patience

If we must be patient with ourselves – our own questions, our own misgivings, our own frustrations – we must be patient with our loved ones, as well – and yes, even our Christian family members and friends. We may at times feel that they are out to invalidate our convictions, but often times I think people are less concerned about what our head covering says about us than what it says about *them*. They may reason that if we feel called to something spiritual that they have no interest in learning about, then we are either crazy or so in tune with devotional matters that it makes them uncomfortable. And sometimes it's easier to believe that we are crazy. If they rebuke or deny our head covering, they deny that anything is amiss in their own relationship with God. If we don't cover, it means *they* are okay. It means there is nothing they need to change. Sometimes people mistake our decision to cover for a finger pointing right at them. When this is not our intent, it hurts to be misunderstood. But our loved ones are navigating their way through this head covering deal just the same as we are. Let's extend them grace by giving them our love and care – not our resentment, anger or withdrawal.

Buckle up. Covering is a wide-eyed ride such as you've never experienced. It's hilly and unpredictable. It's bumpy and winding. But hey, what if God is up to something? What if He is asking us to become something we may not want to rush into being – remarkably *peculiar*? What if He is asking us to be brave enough to do what even the good and religious folks aren't doing? What if He is calling us to walk in the footsteps of a Savior who was more concerned with the condition of the heart than He was about being thought of as weird?

Your True Experience

If you know what you believe, no one can talk you out of it. You don't need to prove it, although you may encounter people who will make you feel as if you must. You needn't apologize for what you are sensing from God. There may be many who will tell you that the I Corinthians 11 passage is no longer intended for today, but it doesn't mean that it's sinful if you decide to cover. There are a million and one rebellious, questionable and sinful things – things not at all becoming of a Christian – which you could pursue if you wanted to. But you didn't opt for any of those. In other words, you could do a whole lot worse than feeling like you want to cover your head. But if something grows you in holiness, leads you to pray more, makes you a better wife, a better mother, a better friend and servant, and draws you closer to Christ – is it *really* so bad? I did all but tell some this one important point: maybe it's not required of me in this day and age, but have I truly sinned if I decide to cover anyway? I certainly don't think so. I think the same can be said of the rest of us, too, providing we aren't walking around thumbing our noses at other women who don't cover. If we are demanding in our desire, we lose the holiness of such a beautiful grace as covering. We don't need to stand up and be heard, nor insist on getting our way. But we do need to know what we believe, and have some sort of good reason why we believe it. When I was a campus minister, I once heard one of my colleagues say, in essence, that you can't argue a sinner into believing, and he might attempt to unravel your theology, but he can never take away your experience. What is happening to you is true and absolutely real. It belongs to you and, even if circumstances prevent you from covering, no one can ever take that away from you.

*C*hapter 13

It Takes a Village to Raise a Movement

Let us not give up meeting together, as some are in the habit of doing, but let us encourage one another – and all the more as you see the Day approaching. – Hebrews 10:25

In my introduction, I said that this was a book I never meant to write. And even as I write this final chapter, I'm aware of the fact that I'm still a bit uncomfortable about writing a book on head covering. I have never thought of myself as a typical church girl. I was saved my freshman year in college while attending a campus Bible study; some of my most meaningful religious experiences have happened *outside* of church, not in it. I would be the woman who best experiences God amidst the beauty of nature, in the narrative of a beautifully woven book, or in a film steeped in redemptive value.

Becoming Sure Again

But something happened between my introduction and this, the final chapter. These women got to me. Sure, I knew I'd be writing about their experiences, and I knew that their experiences were, in many ways, similar to mine, but their narratives weren't just words falling softly on paper. Through their stories, I was sure again. I remembered how I got here. I understood afresh just how real and delicate and timely and so full of grace this whole covering thing is. I'd be lying if I said that writing a book on head covering eliminates every smidgen of doubt and minimizes the challenges of covering in a non-covering family, church and culture. But

96

in the artistry of each woman's story, I felt connected again: connected once more to this beautiful movement that's flowering right beneath my nose.

Thirsty Souls and Tearful Moments

When I first announced on my blog that I'd be writing a book on head covering, and would welcome head covering stories and experiences, I got a healthy response. For obvious reasons, I couldn't include every woman's story, but there seemed no end to the emails I would receive from women who happened upon my blog, and who would tell me how much it encouraged them, or how happy they were to have found another woman who covers. I could sense the urgency in those emails – how very much they needed to connect with another like-minded soul. They refreshed me as much as I did them.

And there were also difficult moments. Some women agreed to participate and share their head covering experiences, but would not respond to my efforts to contact them. Others, who were initially thrilled to be a part of the book, dropped their participation because I am not an Orthodox Christian, and thus the book wouldn't be Orthodox in nature. That one hurt and I wept over it.

Destined for this Journey

But I am thankful, all the more, for those women who put up with my hounding, questioning, re-questioning and frantic 'clarification' emails in order that some other woman out there would be encouraged through the solace of this book. Really, we are not much different from those who haven't the remotest interest in covering. We all want the same things in life, really: to love our families, to be good neighbors, to toss our heads back in deep laughter, to teach our kids good values, and to love God faithfully. Our covering is an extension of who we really are and whom God designed us to be. We were destined for this road, it seems – destined for such a community as this and destined for the courage it takes to keep to this path.

Many Little Deaths

From here, we move onward and upward. Our stories don't end here. We are still being written with the powerful finger of an almighty God for a purpose we can't begin to fathom. We still mop our floors, study for finals, eat while driving, argue with our sister, yell at our kids and long for a nanny. But we are a little braver. We are a little more reflective. We are a little more prayerful. We ask ourselves why on earth God would entrust such a delicate thing to the likes of us, and then we think maybe this is just the beginning of all that God will require of us. Maybe learning to die to ourselves in covering is just one step along the way. Maybe there will be many little deaths God will require of us.

Last night as I was washing dishes, I thought briefly of the other side. What if I had never come to cover? What if I decided that I would just let it go, sweep it under a rug somewhere or let some other activity squeeze the life and the significance out of it? What if I convinced myself that it wasn't real, didn't matter? I stood there, at the kitchen sink, and I thought about it for a minute. No. *No*, I couldn't have let it go. I wouldn't have been able to sleep at night. I know me. I wouldn't have been able to reject it for very long.

Changed Lives

It turns out the same was true for the majority of us – it was meant to dwell among us; it was meant to change our lives; it was meant to make us uncomfortable, to challenge our deeply held views; it was meant to humble us and to make us gentle and to make us women in ways that perhaps we hadn't been before. It was meant to confront us and it was meant to unite us. The old African proverb "It takes a village to raise a child" was beginning to materialize in our midst. Only it wasn't a child we found ourselves raising, but a movement. We weren't looking for a movement or a revolution to join. We just wanted to live quiet, faithful lives for God; but the mere fact that we were experiencing something so out-of-the-ordinary sent us searching for answers. When I first felt led to cover, I went searching for answers. I went looking for a book like this one – a book where the voices of many women could help us better understand that nudging in our spirits. But I never found such a book. I needed to read a book about women just like me: women who were afraid, but who still decided to obey. I wanted (needed!) to know that I was okay. So, with God's help, and the help of several dear sisters, I wrote this book so that you might know that *you* are okay. Or that your sister is okay. Or your wife, or your mother, or your friend.

I couldn't have written this book alone. If there was ever a time when the truth of not being an island unto ourselves rings true, that time is now; it is the moment we hear the call and realize that we must cover. We found out that we need one another. Simply put, this is just too difficult a journey to do alone. There is just not that much support out there in much of the Christian community, to say nothing of the secular world. If we are to do this, and do it well – to do it faithfully, with reverence and with joy – we need a sisterhood; a community where we can grow, ask questions, voice our differences and seek understanding; a village where we are encouraged, affirmed, valued and loved. Together, we form this community, this village, this oasis. We entrust ourselves to God and we entrust ourselves to one another. It is a safe and beautiful place, and something tells me we will be here for a long, long time.

Bibliography

Henderson, Warren A. *Glories Seen and Unseen: A Study of the Head Covering*. Living
   Stone Bookshop Limited, 2002; Warren Henderson, 2007.

Shank, Tom. *"...Let Her Be Veiled.": An In Depth Study of I Corinthians 11:1-16*. Eureka, MT: Torch Publications, 1992.

Williams, Paul K. *The Head Coverings of 1 Corinthians 11*. Eshowe, South Africa: Paul Williams, 2005.
   <http://www.headcoverings.org/>.

Blogs of Women Featured in Life as a Prayer*
(These blogs may contain links to other head covering bloggers, articles and resources.)

Barei Lev (Sanil's blog):
<http://sanilrivka.blogspot.com/>

Head Covering (Sandra's blog) :
<http://headcovering.blogspot.com/>

Homestead Wife in Training (Regina's blog):
<http://www.homesteadblogger.com/coveredwifeoftim>

Little Steps Home (Amber's blog):
<http://littlestepshome.blogspot.com/>

Making Jesus my Pearl (Joanna's blog) :
<http://makingjesusmypearl.blogspot.com/>

Testimony of Grace (Michele's blog):
<http://www.muhala.blogspot.com/>

Those Headcoverings (Lisa's blog):
<http://www.thoseheadcoverings.blogspot.com/>

---

*Isidora does not have a blog.
*Kim does not have a blog.

Head Covering Resources

The Headcovering Directory:
<http://www.headcovering.info/> – Provides
extensive links to various head covering articles,
head covering shops, as well as links to the
stories of other women who share their reasons
for covering.

Those Headcoverings (the resource guide):
<http://thoseheadcoverings.googlepages.com/>
- Provides a wide range of links categorized by
faiths (Christian, Islamic, Jewish, etc.) and
various other resources and articles.

For Further Reading and Study

Calvin, J., Henry, M., Manton, T., et al. (1994).
 Head Coverings and Women. Edmonton,
 Alberta, Canada: Still Waters Revival Books,
 1994.

Campbell, R.K. *Headship and Head Covering:
 According to Scripture*. Sunbury, PA:
 Believers Bookshelf, 1984.

Horst, Myron. *Myths About the Head Covering*.
Biblical Research Reports.

<http://www.biblicalresearchreports.com/headc
overingmyths.php>

Terry, Bruce. *"No Such Custom" – An Exposition
of 1 Corinthians 11:2-16.* Second Edition.
Montezuma Creek, UT: Christian Messenger
Publishers, 1983.
<http://www.ovc.edu/terry/articles/headcovr.htm>.

Head Covering and Modest Attire

Artizara - <http://www.artizara.com/>.

Candle on the Hill -
<http://www.candleonthehill.net/store/pages/h
eadcoveringtips.php>.

Capsters - <https://www.capsters.com/>.

Cover Your Hair -
<http://www.coveryourhair.com/>.

Drawn Together by Modesty - <http://drawn-
together-by-modesty.com/>.

Garlands of Grace -
<http://www.garlandsofgrace.com/>.

Modest Clothing Directory -
<http://www.modestclothes.com/>.

Plain –n- Simple Headcoverings -
<http://www.prayercoverings.com/>.

The Hair Covering Store -
<http://www.haircoverings.com/>.

Tzius - <http://www.tznius.com/>.

104

Made in the USA
Lexington, KY
14 May 2013